WORSHIP

The Alabaster Box Experience

Copyright© 2018 Angel Miller Barrino, Angel B. Inspired Inc.

Unless otherwise indicated all scripture references are from the King James Version, New International Version, English Standard Versions of the Bible and a few verses from the Message Bible, used by permission. Scripture quotations are from the ESV® Bible (The Holy Bible, English Standard Version®), copyright © 2001 by Crossway, a publishing ministry of Good News Publishers. Used by permission. All rights reserved.

THE HOLY BIBLE, NEW INTERNATIONAL VERSION® NIV® Copyright © 1973, 1978, 1984 by International Bible Society® Used by permission. All rights reserved worldwide.

All rights reserved. No part of this book may be reproduced (except by the co-authors), stored in any electronic system, or transmitted in any form by any means, without written permission from the publisher and primary author, except for the use of brief quotations in reviews. The publisher gives express permission for each author to use their testimonials in reviews, promotions but not to be reproduced in any other publication.

Individual author contact information is provided within each chapter.

ISBN: 978-0-692-06682-9

Printed in the USA

TABLE OF CONTENTS

ACKNOWLEDGEMENTS iii
FOREWORD v
INTRODUCTION 1
THE ANOINTING AT BETHANY 3
WONDERFULLY RELEASED 19
FACING MY GIANTS ON THE BATTLEFIELD WITH GOD 24
THE OIL THAT ERASES 35
CHILDREN ARE A GIFT FROM GOD; YEAH RIGHT! 41
BROKEN BUT MENDING 52
I AM HEALED 61
TRAUMA TRINKETS TURNED TO WORSHIP TREASURE 70
THE ROAD LEAST TAKEN 76
THE EXPERIENCE OF A LIFETIME 82
MY BOX OF ALABASTER 91
IN CONCLUSION 98

"And they overcame him by the blood of the Lamb, and by the word of their testimony; and they loved not their lives unto the death."

~Revelations 12:11

SPECIAL DEDICATION

This book is in honor of my Paternal Grandparents: Paul and Louise Miller who were married for 50 years prior to my grandfather's death; my aunts & uncles: Mary Minor, Eddie Minor, Geraldine Moore, Clementine Jones, Isaiah Miller, Daisy Miller, Steve Miller, Martha Miller, James Miller; and beloved cousins who have departed this earthly existence. The love they shared with me, along with the love and support of those who are still with me, propels me forward with divine purpose, passion, and faith.

Worship: The Alabaster Box Experience is also dedicated to those who understand the heartbeat of the Father, particularly His beloved daughters; His provision and His desire for His children to live an abundant life. Through worship and honor of Him, this book project was birthed. From many challenges we have become victorious and better worshippers of Him, recognizing Him as Shepherd, Father, Provider, Protector, Savior and Sovereign King.

And a special dedication to my brother and friend Anthony Price, who always believed in me; he encouraged and supported my writing from elementary school until his departure from this earthly existence this past February 2018. My heart is overjoyed and grateful for having such a good friend & brother who I genuinely considered family.

ACKNOWLEDGMENTS

I am eternally thankful for the goodness, mercy, and favor Abba Father bestows upon my life; His unfailing love and kindness towards me is immeasurable. Without Him, I would be nothing. This has been a journey, and I have grown through it all. My life is so much better with Him than it could ever be without Him. I am so grateful for His provision, protection, and power to be just who He is.

To the woman who is my sister-friend and business bestie, Elder Desireé Harris-Bonner: I love you, and I am so grateful for our hearts and spirits being knitted together spiritually to bring forth anointed and powerful projects which bless the world. Thank you so much for believing in me and this vision. My heart is grateful to you for all you have done to support me and my business. The anointing on your life to bring forth is simply phenomenal. I have learned so much from you, and I am thankful.

To each contributing author: Thank you for sharing your gift of writing, which has come alive through these pages. Your life messages are being shared with many, and I am honored you believed enough in this project to present them here. Your strength is made perfect in weakness. You did it, you pushed through, and you shared your testimony despite your fears or apprehension. The Kingdom and others will surely be blessed through your writing.

To my family and friends: Thank you for your love and support which helps me endure. For every season of my life, many of you have walked with me – Abba Father has blessed me with the gifts of close friendships, family, and mentors who encourage, inspire, motivate and propel me higher. For my parents, daughter, sisters, brothers, nieces, and nephews, grandmother, aunts, uncles, cousins and close beloved friends I love you eternally and I am so blessed to have the gift of love and support. You push me to be better.

To Apostle Janet: Your spiritual wisdom, insight, and guidance has assisted me in fulfilling my purpose through ministry. You believed in me when other leaders wouldn't, and I am so honored and grateful to call you my "spiritual mom." Thank you!

To my companion: Your loving support has been amazing over the last three years. We have faced tremendous obstacles, yet we have grown stronger through it all. I trust the Most High for His purposes in our lives and look forward to what shall come. You see the best and worst of me, yet you still love me. Thank you!

To the readers and customers: You make writing and publishing worth it. If not for you sharing, reading, buying and believing we would not be here. Thank you.

FOREWORD

I can remember hearing the song "*I got a testimony*" by Rev. Clay Evans. The words of the song say:

> "*Sometimes I couldn't see my way through. But the Lord, He bought me out. Right now I'm free. I've got the victory. I've got a testimony.*"

I am sure that we can all relate to this statement at one point or another in our lifetime. I can think back to when things were dark in my world with one setback after another; times when I really couldn't see my way through, reaching out in the dark, and trusting that I was going to grab ahold of God's unchanging hand, while believing the report of the Lord even though I couldn't see any reason to believe.

At the end of my process, I realized that Most High was filling my alabaster box with the oil of the anointing in the midst of the trial. Then He broke it open and poured it out on His people through my testimony.

The Orchestrator and one of the Authors of this powerful book series, Angel M. Barrino is a living testimony herself. Life has taken her through some low valleys, but her faith caused her to never give up, but persevere. The Unmerited Favor and Divine Provision that she has received in times of hardship is evident in her steadfast determination to rise above unfavorable situations.

Testify is dripping with the Oil of Victory.

Not only is this book a testimony of the tenacity that she encompasses, but it is also a record of events in others' lives that to some it may have seemed hopeless, but to the Authors of this awesome compilation of Testimonies, it was just an opportunity for the effectual working of the Arm of God in the earth on their behalf.

The readers are reminded that we are more than conquerors through Him who loved us. **Testify** is evidence of the power to overcome that we possess through the blood of the Lamb and the word of our testimony. Also, being undisputed proof that all things work together for good to them that love God, to them who are the called according to His purpose.

As you read this book, you will come to the realization that there is hope... that you can make it. After experiencing how the Father has delivered and brought the writers out of perilous situations and times, you will begin to rejoice right along with them. We often see people and how they are used by Most High, yet we hardly ever count the cost. The Oil is very costly, and the press is real. However, in the end, not only do you have a testimony, but the Oil of the Anointing is pure. The Writers are real. And, the Stories are real.

Testify Saints, we smell the fragrance of Holy Oil!

Dr. Janet L. Newell D.CLC, D.HU, MCC, BCA
CEO & Chancellor, Rehoboth International Bible College
Author: *Life's Paths, My Little Prophet Manual, Our Weapons Are Not Carnal* and *Put on The Whole Armor of Yahweh*
Sr. Pastor/Apostle & Visionary – The Gathering at Yeshiva Worship International; Wake Forest, NC
www.gatheringatyeshivaworship.org
www.rehobothinternationalbiblecollege.com

INTRODUCTION

As you peruse this book of phenomenal testimonials, you will find that many of these women have penned their personal stories about the Alabaster Box using the biblical account as their foundation, hence their opening statements and titles.

Although similar, the accounts vary as each lady correlates her story to the popular song by CeCe Winans and the Bible illustration of worship: The Anointing of Jesus at Bethany.

The theme of Alabaster resonates throughout this book of course, with good reason because women are being broken, poured out, healed and restored, as they commit to becoming conduits for the Kingdom for such a time as this. Purposefully, I have not added an Alabaster Box testimony as I wanted the women to openly share their experiences. However, the last five years of compiling this amazing trilogy have been captured and summarized in the final pages, so that you will understand what this prophetic legacy has meant for me... and each contributor.

Receive your healing. Do not just read the words, internalize them and allow them to penetrate your soul, spirit, and heart. Let Holy Spirit permeate you with His power of restoration and revival, leading you back to where you belong in Him. As the oil and anointing of the Most High flows, feel and trust His presence to heal you. This is your moment. And it has been set aside just for you to embrace **Worship: *The Alabaster Box Experience.***

Angel B. & the Praise Literary Collection Team

THE ANOINTING AT BETHANY
MINISTER NELLIE A. WOSU

"A woman came to Him having an alabaster flask of very costly fragrant oil, and she poured it on His head as He sat at the table. But when His disciples saw it, they were indignant, saying, 'Why this waste? For this fragrant oil might have been sold for much and given to the poor.'

But when Jesus was aware of it, He said to them, 'Why do you trouble the woman? For she has done a good work for Me. For you have the poor with you always, but Me you do not have always. For in pouring this fragrant oil on My body, she did it for My burial. Assuredly, I say to you, wherever this gospel is preached in the whole world, what this woman has done will also be told as a memorial to her.'" ~ Matthew 26:7-13 (NKJV)

In today's world, we don't often think of our lives as being reflective of days of old. However, we understand, that Scripture tells us that there is nothing new under the sun. In fact, there never was, and there will never be anything new under the sun, for any of us. Until the day comes where those of us who are written in the Lamb's Book of Life, will see the new life and the Son of God, in all His glory.

Seems afar off at times. We hope for it. We pray for it. We believe for it. But, most often, we are afraid of it, that it will come, and we'll not be ready. How unfortunate that would be and actually is. Living in these recent centuries, we've become, I suppose, numbed to true tribulation and trial. James tells us to 'count it all joy,' well, we're not always doing that. Certainly, I haven't, even when I've known to do so. And, believe me, I do know to do so. Am I that wretched man (includes women, also) that Paul speaks about when he says, 'what I will to do, I do not, and what I will not to do, that is what I do.'

We're in turmoil even in peace times.

Much happens in the world as it always has, but then again, there is much that is even unspeakable happening in our lives. Both daily life and perhaps even life that has long been over, for some reason continues to keep on. The shadows of this life that have certainly run their course, well it appears that they are seen in daylight. They continue to berate us with what was. We, being the humans that we are, forget to put things behind us and press on to the higher prize. Try as we may, we falter in not being able to finish this and stay on higher ground.

Why? It's in us to not believe that we're truly forgiven. However, we have been forgiven. The truth of all matters in our lives resides with Him, and Him alone. There is no condemnation in Him, and there never will be.

The woman spoken of in the Scripture referenced above is me at times, and at times on many levels. Yet, I do know within me, that I'm forgiven beyond compare and loved too. Something lingers in me. Shadows of the past. I am at times too pre-occupied with the past. No, I don't permit it to hold me back. I go there and reflect, not to review and or see, where He's brought me from, but to enter the pain again, and even at times, to "see" new pain, in various matters that occur in present time.

Have you been guilty of that? Listen, you don't have to tell me about it, I know about it. But, tell yourself you're doing it. Put yourself on notice and get it right. So, you can go on and be the victorious individual that you are and always have been whether you believe it or not. Simply put you have been created for greater. Have you heard that your latter will be greater than your former? It is in His word which concerns all of us, and that includes you to my brothers and sisters.

There's a story that I will share with you now. First, I want to examine that portion of the Scripture above and see how it identifies, fits and reveals a truth about me. If you care to, you may also try this exercise for your *self* and story. I hope that in time you will reconsider the situations in your life... past, present, and future. I have been doing so, and this opportunity to share my story has come at an integral point as a reminder and lightning bolt jolt causing me to rise up and give thanks for the tribulation in the tribulation.

Please note that I am a Minister of the Gospel of Jesus Christ. However, as a Minister, some often think that we will escape the wrath of daily living. Not so, we may quite often be tested more. No matter what position we are in life, it matters not.

What matters is that humanity will be engaged by trials and tribulation. Just as there is nothing new under the sun, we must also realize and know, that there is a time and season for everything. Life is seemingly not always fair to us.

When we think about that and say that, I can see, heads nodding up and down, up and down in agreement. Will there be a nodding of our own head up and down, up and down, when we begin to think of the unfair ways we've engaged Life (notice I used an initial capital letter "L" for life). I am referencing God, for He is the truth, the Light, and the Life. In the Good Book, it's stated as such:

Jesus said to him, "I am the way, the truth, and the life.
No one comes to the Father except through Me."
~ John 14:6

Prior to that truth, I want to implore you to accept this about you and all of the situations that have been, are and will be in your life, all of them, equally today and beyond. My prayer is for you to go higher and see a new you, with your vision restored all for His glory.
Check this out:

> *"All that the Father gives Me will come to Me, and the one who comes to Me I will by no means cast out."*
> ~ John 6:37

That, my friend, is a promise from Jesus. We are all the one in the ninety-nine. He is here for us. Accept it, thankfully and humbly, but knowing boldly that that's just the way it is. Nothing in your past or present circumstances can equal the good things that have been prepared for you.

The total truth is that we are the only ones who can abort the blessings and provisions by not understanding His truth. And, if you're thinking that you're not that spiritual to receive same, then ask Him to help you in your unbelief and to show you the way of rising up all for His glory.

Your story will encourage someone today, and every day which also includes, you, I pray. I've found that when I am at my lowest point where ever that may fall on the number line, it's good to go in and help another, then most times, in those matters I've found that I'm more than blessed beyond measure, I'm blessed beyond compare!

What it is, not what it could be. Life has taught me this, "the weapon that is formed against me, I ought not to let it (the weapon) be found in my own hand."

The enemy cannot destroy you. Unless you believe what the enemy says, and we do know that the enemy is not only a lie, but a liar as well. Get the picture?

My Mother taught me that the truth will stand, and a lie will fall. You have more resources and power than what you believe, realize and more importantly tap into and use to not only bless you but others.

I have found that I am more of the above. However, the person that I am, I generally do it more for others than I do it for myself. No, I'm not an over sacrificing type of person. If I love you, I'm going to do everything in my power to help make it as right as I can for you.

Here's where we begin with my story and perhaps your own, even. How much do you truly love yourself? Do you believe your true worth? Or, do you believe all of that for others and not for yourself? Remember, the first law of nature is self-preservation. My Uncle Herbert, who is now a retired Science teacher, explained that to me as a young child.

As I was taking my first airplane ride, it came clear to me, when the Flight Attendant, explained about the necessity of caring for yourself before moving to assist another. I've flown so many times since then, I've never heard a change in that statement which is truth. Life has afforded me many more opportunities to see this in action. So, tell me why, I've reneged in doing so for my betterment?

A type of fear of being the great one that I am, is one reason. Not wanting to cause anyone anger, angst or any other untruth to feel that I'm thinking I am all of that.

Truth be told I AM ALL OF THAT. Not, in a gloating manner, but it is written, about me. I do come in the volume of the book that it is written of me, as do you!

So, the story goes as such...

A Sinful Woman Forgiven

> Then one of the Pharisees asked Him to eat with him. And He went to the Pharisee's house, and sat down to eat. And behold, a woman in the city who was a sinner, when she knew that Jesus sat at the table in the Pharisee's house, brought an alabaster flask of fragrant oil, and stood at His feet behind Him weeping; and she began to wash His feet with her tears, and wiped them with the hair of her head; and she kissed His feet and anointed them with the fragrant oil.
>
> Now when the Pharisee who had invited Him saw this, he spoke to himself, saying, "This Man, if He were a prophet, would know who and what manner of woman this is who is touching Him, for she is a sinner." And Jesus answered and said to him, "Simon, I have something to say to you."
>
> So he said, "Teacher, say it."
>
> "There was a certain creditor who had two debtors. One owed five hundred denarii, and the other fifty. And when they had nothing with which to repay, he freely

forgave them both. Tell Me, therefore, which of them will love him more?"

Simon answered and said, "I suppose the one whom he forgave more." And He said to him, "You have rightly judged." Then He turned to the woman and said to Simon, "Do you see this woman? I entered your house; you gave Me no water for My feet, but she has washed My feet with her tears and wiped them with the hair of her head. You gave Me no kiss, but this woman has not ceased to kiss My feet since the time I came in. You did not anoint My head with oil, but this woman has anointed My feet with fragrant oil. Therefore I say to you, her sins, which are many, are forgiven, for she loved much. But to whom little is forgiven, the same loves little."

Then He said to her, "Your sins are forgiven."

And those who sat at the table with Him began to say to themselves, "Who is this who even forgives sins?"
Then He said to the woman, "Your faith has saved you. Go in peace." (Luke 7:36-50)

I am that Sinful Woman. Yes, me, a Minister, Teacher, you name it. I am she. Love generally has been the instigator of my being sinful, my need and desire to be loved by my significant other, which would become my spouse.

Twice.

My need/desire is not a result of my not loving myself. I love my self but with limits that I don't place or require of others. I have a healthy sense of confidence in myself. What I do is sacrifice myself far more than is needed or required because "I love you." I've been left alone, feeling abandoned yet again, and maybe thinking that I am not good enough, yet?

Truth be told, I am crying in this moment, right now, thinking about the sadness of it all. I preach, stand on the soapbox to empower others to not fall into these type traps. No, I don't fall into them. I surely do not. What I do, is just go in and step on down into the traps, again, not thinking of what this means to me. I am not the Savior. I am in need of being saved. I've placed all in for love. Back in the day, there was a song that used to literally spin me off which said, "I'll do ANYTHING FOR YOU. I'LL GIVE THE WORLD TO YOU, IF YOU WANT ME TO. YES, I WILL."

So sad. I was in my early 20s with that noose around my neck. No, I don't do stupid extremes, but I certainly go out of my way. Again, I say beyond what is necessary. I love deeply and completely. This has been me not just in love matters, but in even in my personal relationships, as well.

The question to and for you and me may use it as well. Why haven't I dedicated and sacrificed this much for Father, Son, and Holy Ghost? Why is it that I've given myself over to Christ, but how much and for how long? It's not equal; it's not fair. I know that. I know that. I know that! The Lord has been my Redeemer, My Keeper (I wrote a book about that truth), my

Salvation and my Life but I still did not sacrifice as much for my Lord as I did for others.

I was a Daddy's girl, and perhaps that is why I love so hard. What I've learned is that to love, is to give beyond measure. Sacrifice, never mind, how it may leave you. Not trying to buy anyone, but encouraging beyond measure and never, ever, seeming to get a kind reply that *yes, you've done a good thing, thank you so much, Anita.*

One loved of mine had dogged me out beyond anything necessary. Called me out. Told me that they hated me. Humph, really? Then, in less than twenty-four hours they came to me and asked me for some serious money. Shocked? No, that's what the enemy does to you through others, at times. Me questioning the loved one, "thought you said you hate me."

Their response? *"I do, but I don't hate your money."*

How are we to navigate something as hurtful as that? My eyes were full of tears and my heart was heaving heavily, pounding inside the cavity of the center of the life in me. I should have said to that friend of mine, "get behind me satan."

It's not often that we actually engage ourselves to do a soul searching to have a come to Jesus meeting with the activities that we permit in our lives. I've found that the hurts that have hurt me the most, were caused by me. I've gone above and beyond for others. Do they appreciate what I've done? Sometimes it may be difficult to face the truth. Who wants to face the question 'will a man rob God?' to me this is not financially.

I constantly rob God of my time with Him. Yes, I love Him more that can be believed or even expressed. The answer is yes; I've robbed Him, not given Him His just time, involved with this or that. Instead of coming to Him on a totally regular basis, to keep me balanced in my heart. The Lord is the only Person who loves me without judgment, without being jealous, without giving side-eye foolishness. He also doesn't let me get away with non-sense. I wish we could have a moment to sit face-to-face to talk more effectively about this crucial issue.

Many years ago, 27 years as of 2017, my mother transitioned without any hint that she was about to be finished in this realm. She had a triple bypass. It was thought that she would be up and about like a champ. Well, she was up and about like a champ, but not in this realm. Her procedure was performed, and she transitioned less than 24 hours later, on what would have been her 30th wedding anniversary.

My Father had preceded her two decades before.

The point to be made here is that I hadn't given her, her just dues as a daughter. I had been overly encumbered with trying to make a go out of my relationship with my former spouse.

If it hadn't been for her call one day, and something inside me saying, "When she gets here, be ready to take yourself and the baby and stay with her for a few." I did, and at least, I have that as a comfort. I was blessed to be in her company without being distracted by crap. I got to see her engage with my daughter, the way she used to engage me when I was a little girl.

My daughter was three years old, so her and Grandma, would go to the park and have fun. Just like she and I used to do. As always Mommy made my breakfast every morning before I went to work. What if that time during a difficult time was not afforded to me and my daughter? There were distractions beyond speaking about. What if I didn't heed this opportunity to go and be comforted?

Comforted, you say? Yes, I say, comforted.

Out of a terrible situation, the slow dissolution of our marriage, Jesus, provided me with an opportunity to be loved, and receive love unhindered, and to see love grow again in my daughter and me. I gave my earthly parent, her just dues, and in doing so. I prayerfully will not take it lightly to engage my heavenly Father in being His daughter and learn from Him, what is needed in me now as a middle-aged woman.

It's more imperative than ever for me to engage Him. He's into me so why, do, I not enter into Him all the more? The sin against Him has been to not place Him first and foremost above everything, and most certainly above everyone. Even being a good parent and forsaking our heavenly Father is disobedience and sinful. In His word of Commandments to us, we've been told to have no other gods before Him.

I am guilty of that. Shamefully. Intimacy with our heavenly Parent is what is required to achieve any semblance of balance in the other areas of our lives. He is the only One that gives us anything worthwhile. He gives us His life every moment of every moment. We are absolutely nothing without Him. I've learned that He must get my absolute entire self before anyone.

In my last relationship, with my significant other, for over twenty years, we finally married. I was completely engaged in my work in ministry for my Father's glory, and when I am immersed... I am immersed. I felt a deep satisfaction of being in service to the Lord. After a period of time, my former spouse, I believe, began to feel left out. When I explained to him that nothing at all mattered to me but God, I soon found the marriage crumbling at breakneck speed.

He disengaged, he went silent, and he went to work and kept on trucking. I saw him 16 months later. My heart was weak and sick and joyful at the same time. My heart rejoiced that I had stuck with God. God never leaves me, and He never will.
Priorities in life are difficult to navigate. There's a delicate balance to achieve. However, we must engage God to obtain the proper balance in this life.

What's new is to ask God to assist us in the ways that enable us to balance our lives. Take everything to God in prayer. Don't ask jealous girlfriends; they're too envious, wondering how you're able to manage and do the impossible without the flash of cash. It's called favor from God. God made the ram and the bush. He is my way maker. He is my miraculous heart restorer, He is my breath, in essence, and "He is The Keeper of Me."

Today, I went to the house of the Lord, and I was introduced to Him yet again, and this time, I know how to keep the most important relationship that I'll ever have and that I've ever had in the proper way. That is to have no other God's before Him.

I must work at doing what I am gifted to do, and that is, to be about my Father's business, and forgetting about mine.

My sins are many; Lord have mercy on me. Now, finally, finally, finally, I am at and in peace. Why should I not serve Him all the days of my life? The days which He has given me, for I am His daughter. My full faith, trust, and belief must be in and because of Him. Let's not block our blessings by not placing God first in everything in the life that He's given to us, and that includes first the giving of His life for YOU & Me!

He has said this about me:

> "Therefore, I say to you, her sins, which are many, are forgiven, for she loved much. But to whom little is forgiven, the same loves little."
>
> Then He said to her, "Your sins are forgiven."
>
> And those who sat at the table with Him began to say to themselves, "Who is this who even forgives sins?"

Then He said to the woman, "Your faith has saved you. Go in peace."

"But without faith it is impossible to please Him, for he who comes to God must believe that He is, and that He is a rewarder of those who diligently seek Him." (Hebrews 11:6)

Then He said to Nellie Anita, *"Your faith has saved you. Go in peace."* Thanks, be unto You, my Lord Jesus Christ! I pour my oil of thanksgiving upon You with gladness in my heart all the days of my life. *"Assuredly, I say to you, wherever this gospel is preached in the whole world, what this woman has done will also be told as a memorial to her"* (Matthew 26:13).

Minister Nellie A. Wosu is a National Spokesperson & Champion for WomenHeart: The National Coalition for Women with Heart Disease, the nation's only patient advocacy organization headquartered in Washington, DC. Nellie is also a patient spokesperson for national health agenda Measure Up Pressure Down.

Minister Wosu was referenced in an article in the March 2013 Edition of ESSENCE Magazine concerning the impact of stress upon today's woman. Also, in December 2012, Wosu penned her journey with heart disease entitled *"The Keeper of Me"* an Amazon Best Seller, published by **Gatmoon Publishing, L.L.C.** located in Concord, North Carolina of which she is the Publisher & CEO. She is the owner of NWN Radio & Television Broadcasting on the WWW streaming from SIBN.NET.

Minister Wosu is not only surviving with heart disease she is thriving and encourages others to do the same with their health journey. Nellie believes the disease has propelled her into her life's mission and purpose for His glory to benefit many perhaps even including you!

Minister Wosu is also a contributing author for the second book in this series, *Unmerited Favor & Divine Provision*.

Contact her at: **www.gatmoonpublishing.com**

WONDERFULLY RELEASED
PASTOR BJ RELFOURD

A southern lady always carries herself with class and a flair which reflects the gentleness of waves flowing over the ocean.

This southern lady has truly witnessed the stern and disciplined instruction that should have given each of the young'uns at the time a warning not to become entangled or involved with anything that would cause the family name to be questioned or dishonored.

How lovely it was to sit on the porch and try my best to hear the conversations of the matriarchs and patriarchs sharing anecdotes of wisdom and humor. While my knowledge of the dialogue was limited, I was intrigued with what appeared to be so interesting, that the tones would change to whispers as we, the young ones grew closer to the railing on the front porch. What is absolutely humorous now is that I didn't know the front porch was the courtroom, it was also the jury box where deliberations were held, and the front porch was also the judge's chambers.

The continuation or demise of relationships were weighed on the front porch. Decisions which were life-altering were made in the rocking chairs, which were many on the front porch. The wave of a hand fan, the scrunch of eyebrows, and the turn of a head were acts which proclaimed guilt or innocence in the lives of those discussed.

I often wondered, how could I possibly fit in? How would I ever be in a position to live up to their expectations? Surely at one time or another, I had been the subject of the conversation. Knowingly or unknowingly, had I been found guilty of the raging saga of the past, even when I had no idea of the depth of the hidden story?

The fragile box of history I brought with me to this grand occasion was one which was never discussed, at least not in my presence; however, there was a pulling within me that told me, I was different. As my large inquisitive eyes roamed the porch, the yard, the family, I questioned, "Why does no one look like me?" I viewed the similarities in the facial features and body structures of those whom we knew as family.

I waited anxiously when family members would travel from "up north" to our southern residence for the annual family reunion, a loved one's wedding and sadly, of course, the transition of a beloved relative. Year after year there was never an arrival of an individual who in any way appeared to have any of the facial features I had, nor me having any of theirs.

Always inquisitive and eager to learn, my quest for research increased. Not known for being the greatest mathematician, I had to research the current age of my parents at the time, in reference to my age. Unless the great matriarch I knew had a miraculous conception, this could not be!

What had I uncovered? Did I just open a can of worms which now could never be concealed again?

No one told me not to discuss what was now being revealed to me, but for some reason, I knew this was to be concealed information, so I closed the box filled with this valuable yet disturbing information. Valuable because this knowledge gave some credibility to the fact, I wasn't being overly sensitive to the differences I viewed. Yet, disturbing for now and armed with the data, what would I do with it? How far would I investigate and dissect the facts which would ultimately prove me to be an outsider?

Did I really want to know?

I share the backdrop of this story so that you can recognize the characteristics of those who become overachievers. I allow a glimpse into the window of one who determined at an early age that I would be the best little girl in the family—the most intelligent teen they could ever imagine. By doing so, this great family would never want me to leave; they would always welcome me as their own. They would never know I knew the difference.

This information would lie tucked neatly away in my box, and my quest for perfection would continue to go forth.

Sadly, those unrealistic goals took a toll, and I turned to alcohol to numb the void of unanswered questions and conversations which never took place. Overwhelmed with inquiries and genealogy which would lead me to the source of who I really was, became painstakingly a mission pursued with a vengeance.

It was the precious gift of the Holy Spirit which released me from the bondage and the incarceration of the box of inquiries, and questions which after being answered, never made a difference anyway. I learned to "praise the Lord, for I was fearfully and wonderfully made, and I know this full well." (Psalms 139:14)

Coming to the realization that my source of conception, never negated my point of completion. I am complete because Christ lives within me. I was conceived and placed in an atmosphere that never caused me to feel inadequate; that was the plan of the enemy to cause me to feel insecure.

I've learned over the years that being different is not always negative; it just is what it is, different.

I welcome you to open my beautiful alabaster box filled with the precious oils of which I was created, *fearfully and wonderfully made... and I know that full well.*

Pastor BJ Relefourd, "The Lady Leader" is a General in the Kingdom and a gift to the Body of Christ; she is sold out and has a submitted life as unto the Lord. The powerful anointing upon her life leads sinners to Christ, delivers hope, and a yoke-destroying Word to set the captive free. Nearly 30 years of ministry has prepared and purposed her assignment in the Kingdom.

She is the Pastor and Co-Founder of Vision of Life Ministries, Co-Founder of Vision Alliance Ministerial Institute, Founder and visionary of Women of Power, as well as Executive Director of the WOP Network. She utilizes her communication skills by hosting Walking in Power Blog Talk Radio, as well as being the Executive Editor and founder of The Acts of Women of Power Magazine. She's also found on most social outlets.

As a Best-Selling Author and key-note messenger, she utilizes the apostolic Five-fold anointing upon her life to bless an international audience. Pastor BJ also writes a monthly blog—*The Lady Is a Leader*—and is a Luminary on the *Inspire Me Today Network*. The evangelist ministry, *Words of Wisdom* allows her the liberty to travel extensively and serve humbly and effectively.

Her heart is to deliver healing, hope, and the love of Christ to all.

Ordained under the leadership of PHIPA - Potter's House International Pastoral Alliance - Bishop T.D. Jakes, she holds a Doctorate in Theology.

However, after giving her life to the Lord, Pastor BJ holds most dearly being the wife of over 34 years to her high school sweetheart, Rev. Marion Relefourd, and being the mother and nana of the Relefourd family.

Contact her at:
Email: pastorbj@women-of-power.org
Website: www.pastorbj.org | www.women-of-power.org

FACING MY GIANTS ON THE BATTLEFIELD WITH GOD
REV. LILLIAN DUNBAR

There was a time when I felt like a complete failure. I share this information with you because, like many, I have felt haunted by the mistakes of my past.

Reflecting on something I read in a magazine years ago, I remember the article stating, "By the age of twenty-six, everyone should know which direction their lives and careers should go." At that time, I did not know and believed my past dictated my future.

Why did I feel this way?

Well, after reading my story, you will understand why.
Society dictates the path that we should follow to become successful in life. Often, we search for strategies through a variety of resources regarding life from birth, as we make many choices. Certainly, there are times that we can benefit from the wisdom gleaned from our fellow man; however, the Bible asks us, "What good will it be for someone to gain the whole world, yet forfeit their soul?" (Matthew 16:26 NIV).

It is through the wisdom of God that we are sustained in this life and eternity to come.

Allow me to continue… As a child, I grew up in the church. I prayed every night to God, but I did not yet have a personal relationship with Him. My parents were very strict, and my knowledge outside of family and church was minimal. I was naïve, and as a teenager, I became pregnant, becoming an outcast in society as a result. During those years, marriage was the decent thing to do when faced with this situation, so that's what we did.

And, I dropped out of school, taking on the role of an adult although I still had a child's heart and mind. The only person I had to express my sincere thoughts with was my gynecologist during regular visits. Yes, I was ashamed of my situation, knowing that I had disappointed both my parents and myself. I also stopped attending church; however, I never ceased praying. My old schoolmates and neighborhood friends could no longer associate themselves with me because I was considered a *bad influence*. Thankfully, I still had my cousins, Sandra and Dorothy, who were around my age.

Daily I questioned the Lord, "Why me?" I felt as if God was punishing me for my mistakes, and I felt all alone in this big world. Nevertheless, I continued to pray to God because there was no one who understood me and my situation.
What could I do? I was a child. It was like a dream that I could not wake up from.

Today, I look at teenagers and imagine myself being pregnant at their age. Oh my God, it blows my mind to think of them being in that situation. How would they make it? What could they do to survive? I made a mistake in life, but I often think to myself, *God, thank you for rescuing me. Lord, I know my situation was a miracle to have survived, and I thank you.* I reflect on Mary, the mother of Jesus and think of the mockery that she faced because of her pregnancy, even though this was God's doing.

It's not a good feeling. It hurts!

My sons were born on Labor Day. I gave birth to a set of healthy, identical twin boys, although they were premature and breech birth. I had experienced the pain for three days. Within two days of delivery, I became ill and remained in the hospital for several weeks. I had lost all strength in my body, could not walk or sit up alone, and had a temperature of 104. The doctors continued to run a variety of tests daily to come up with a solution. From the moment I was admitted to the hospital to the time I was discharged, approximately one month had passed. All my praise was given to God because through this process, He healed me.

Once I returned home, my sisters would sneak to assist me whenever possible with my two babies. They were instructed not to help me because they had their schoolwork and other activities to do. I felt as if my mother thought this was my punishment, and if I realized the toughness of raising these babies, it would not happen again. This experience was hard for me... no sleep due to the twins' schedule and I had anxiety, which I received medicine for. When one slept, the other would be awake and vice versa; however, they were awake to eat together. My father eventually permitted my sisters to help as needed, which was a tremendous relief for me.

My husband and I, along with our boys, moved away to another state fifteen months later. Several years later, we had a precious baby girl. Not long after she was born, we moved to South America. We tried to make the marriage work, but my husband was older, jealous and controlling, and I was young and immature. My life was miserable, and I felt trapped and stressed, while asking myself, *why am I here, what am I going to do, and how can anything good come out of this situation?*

What could I possibly do?

I would often listen to this song, *Thin Line Between Love and Hate* by **The Persuaders**. You would have to hear the words of this song to identify. The time had come for me to make a decision to remain in this situation or to leave because I was fearful and could no longer live this way. Secretly, I saved my money for about a year and had a close girlfriend to go downtown into the city to purchase an airline ticket for me so that I could go back to my parents' home. However, a clearance was required from the military because they were my sponsor while I was overseas in Panama, Canal Zone.

There were many upsetting things to take place before my departure, but it worked out. I flew back to the United States with my three children as my marriage ended. I was young, with no life experience, no education, and no real wisdom of the Lord; still, I believed in my heart, that if God could save and take care of others, then He could do the same for me. I have had some struggles and battles, and I have shed many tears, but I cannot complain because God has been and continues to be good to me, in spite of it all.

Yes, God is faithful and has taken good care of my three children and me! It was many years after, I continued to ask the Lord, "Why me?" Praise God, I don't ask this question any longer because I found His reply:

> *"For I know the plans I have for you,' declares the LORD,*
> *'plans to prosper you and not to harm you,*
> *plans to give you hope and a future."*
> *~ Jeremiah 29:11 NIV*

Now that I have a relationship with God and study HIS WORD, I realize God knew that I would mess up, and He knew the route that I would take to get where I needed to be. "We rejoice in our sufferings, knowing that suffering produces endurance (Romans 5:3 ESV).

God gives us second chances and more, but most of all, He does not give up on us, regardless of the situation(s). The question is, do we have the courage to face the challenges of repeatedly starting to get on the path that God will have you to travel? I believe sometimes we must go down into the valley to get to the mountaintop; only to learn that it is not society's (the people's) opinion that matters, but the plans that God has for us.

As a child, to include adulthood, I was in search of happiness, yet I could not find it. I wore beautiful clothes to feel better on the outside, but I felt empty on the inside. Each day, I continued smiling—not realizing that I was only existing and not living.

The life I lived was a sinful life while searching for happiness. I continued to have doubts and questions about my situation. Reality set in when my father became diagnosed with cancer in December of 1999 and died a short time later. I prayed daily, asking God for a miracle of healing. I was expecting a miracle, however; it did not happen, I thought. My father died the day after my birthday. The tears rolled from my eyes for years.

My father's death had a major effect upon my family's life. He had held our family together through his strength, guidance, laughter, and love. It took my father's death for me to consider my mortality. I realized that I wanted to see him again one day, and I wondered where I would go in the afterlife.

I will never forget this experience. It was one Saturday morning, January 12, 2002, to be exact. I cried out to the Lord for hours and hours confessing that I needed Him because I could not continue living with pain, shame, uncertainty, and regrets. I was sick and tired of being sick and tired, and I couldn't handle anymore. I shouted out, "I need You and can't go any further without You. I give up." I realized I was on the battlefield and I needed God's help to face my giants of pain and uncertainty. God delivered me to a place of peace, joy, and fulfillment while resting in His presence and at His feet.

It was then that I heard this small still voice from within, telling me to "FOLLOW MY STEPS." It was through the spirit of the Lord I gained my VICTORY. I had been trying to fight my own battles for many years without God, but this time I surrendered my life to HIM. Remember, there will always be a void in your life without GOD.

I often think of my father's death, which occurred during the year of 1999 and the prayer I prayed to God. I thought God did not answer my prayer while expecting a miracle for my father's healing and he died, but God healed my father from the pain and agony and took him to a resting place of peace.

The one supreme revelation of God's love for the lost and His goodness toward humanity is the sacrifice of His only son (John 3:16). How do I know? God changed me, and my testimony changed my path for good in spite of my past mistakes. My soul knows I am called to preach, teach, and encourage others with the Gospel of Jesus Christ to make disciples for Him. I am a licensed and ordained minister. I became an ordained minister on my father's birthday (April 27), God's timing.

> *"Go into all the world*
> *and preach the gospel to all creation."*
> *~ Mark 16:15*

Even though I dropped out of school because of pregnancy, I received my GED later. Since that time, I have attended several years of colleges. I first began studying classes for Criminal Justice, and later, I attended Lee University, graduating with a Bachelor's degree and honors in Biblical Studies in Christian Ministry (Cum Laude). I also graduated with my Master's degree in Christian Leadership Ministry with honors (Magna Cum Laude) and now am currently working on my Doctorate.

Missionary work has afforded me the ability to travel to Ghana, West Africa and Johannesburg, South Africa. I have preached, taught, encouraged, and spoken at women's conferences with the help of the Holy Spirit. I served God's people through the Gospel of Jesus Christ by helping with needed goods in the villages as well. I have traveled to at least 40 of the 50 states.

With God's help, I have been able to volunteer and help many people through my ministry. I have worked with battered women, participated in court advocacy, worked with rape victims, incarcerated individuals, worked in elderly people's homes, with hospice patients, rehabilitation patients, veterans support, volunteered for the Red Cross Bloodmobile, and other community services dealing with crisis.

I have served in the United States Navy Reserve active duty for over ten years and retired from a Federal Government job with thirty-one years of service. Additionally, I teach and preach in the prisons, while leading Bible study to the women in the local jail. To God be the Glory for His love, grace, and mercy.

Honestly, I am blessed in my new life with Christ and the marvelous things that He has done, is doing and is going to do in my life and family! My life experiences have not necessarily fallen in the order and age of most, but God worked it out in His timing. Worshipping and praising Him brought me through it. *If God did it for me, He can do it for you too!*

I hope to encourage women across the world to look forward to God fighting their battles while facing their giants. Many women are facing what seems like hopeless situations, but each day God gives us tokens of His goodness. God's word is mighty, and it is the bringer of life and the giver of hope. He wants to restore His children to the likeness of Himself, through spiritual transformation.

When people gain knowledge of Christ by reading, listening, studying, and meditating on God's Word, it leads to a personal relationship with our heavenly Father. He knows our hearts and our burdens. He will fight our battles.

God has blessed me with three beautiful children, Ron, Don, and Monique. As a single parent, I would pray daily, "God, please let me live to see my children reach the age of eighteen, so no one else will have to take care of them." My sons are now fifty-years-old, and my daughter is forty-seven. I have nine grandchildren and two great-grandchildren. God has granted me years beyond my prayer request.

Many thanks to my children, Ron, Don, Monique, godmother Lottie Stamper, god-sister Pastors Ivory Bostick and her husband, god-brother John, family, and many other God-sent people who have encouraged me during this journey. I thank everyone for their prayers and encouragement along the way. I pray that my story touches someone in need of support.

Remember, God equips us with the gifts needed to do His will and not necessarily our desires. Are you in need of a lifesaving change? *"Trust in the LORD with all your heart and lean not on your own understanding; in all your ways submit to him, and he will make your paths straight."* (Proverbs 3:5-6)

A native of New Orleans, **Lillie Young-Dunbar** was educated in the public schools of Louisiana. She married and ultimately became the mother of three wonderful children, Ronald, Donald, and Monique. In 1969, Lillie transitioned from Louisiana to Virginia. The year of 2005, she accepted her license as an Evangelist minister and was ordained in 2008.

Lillie has continued her education at Lee University with a bachelor's degree in Christian Ministry Biblical Studies, graduating with honors (Cum Laude) and a Master's degree in Christian Leadership Ministry with honors (Magna Cum Laude). She is currently working on her Doctrine's degree at Bethel Seminary.

In 2009, Lillie received the National Association for the Advancement of Colored People (NAACP) award for Community Evangelism. She has dedicated her life as a servant of Christ to help others in need, including the sick, homeless, widows, orphans, and the broken. She daily reminds people that there is power in the name of Jesus and all things are possible through Christ.

Lillie's future goals are publishing a series of books to reach the world for Jesus Christ and to start a Women's Ministry to share the Gospel of Jesus Christ with other women. She was featured in the KISH Magazine in an article, "New Beginnings", and interviewed in The GARNETT NEWSLETTER "A GLORIOUS STROLL IN HIS VINEYARD." The UPWORDS Magazine front covers honoree of December 2017 (edition) and article on serving the community. Magazine in Kolkata, India. Her dreams extend to a hope that will encourage women across the world.

Contact her at:
Facebook: Lillie Dunbar
Email: ldunbar14@yahoo.com

THE OIL THAT ERASES
LADY SIMA CLARK-TORIAN

Have you ever been betrayed? Of course, you have. Isn't it true that betrayal from a family member or your closest friend is by far the most difficult kind of betrayal to not only digest but to move forward from?

Let's face it, betrayal, unfortunately, is only bred from close relationships. Betrayal from a stranger holds little to no weight in the grand scheme of things. As a matter of fact, betrayal cuts deep to the bone. Unfortunately, we can't escape it. None of us can.

When I think of an alabaster box, I think of "stone commonly found in Israel. It was a hard stone resembling white marble used in the decoration of Solomon's Temple (I Chronicles 29:2). When oil is stored in an alabaster box, it is kept "pure and unspoiled." At the appropriate time, the box is opened, and the essence and fragrance of the oil are released. But, until then, it's kept pure and without blemish.

When I think of oil, I am immediately reminded of the process by which to extract oil from an olive. There is a process that includes grinding, crushing and pressing. The olive goes through this process in order to extract the best of the olive for the oil and leaving the impurities behind. The key here is understanding that to get the oil, there must be pressing. The pressing is required to extract the oil.

Beloved, God allows the pressing to release the oil in you. He allows the grinding to propel you to release your oil. He allows the crushing to create a space for oil to flow.

As aforementioned, pressure is necessary for proper processing of the oil. When was the last time a season of pressing created an oil in your life? I am reminded of a pivotal moment in my Christian walk where God used the pressing to release my own oil. It was a four-year process that seemed like forever. However, while I was being pressed, I had no idea God was preparing my oil.

My day would come, and oil would be released.

Allow me to explain what I mean. Each week for several months, I received threatening phone calls from debt collectors trying to collect a debt on a BMW 740 that was repossessed. Yes, you read that right. It was repossessed. But, here is the kicker; I did not buy this vehicle. I did not walk into a dealership to purchase it. I never graced the dealership where it had been purchased. I never signed my name to agree to the contract.

You may be thinking, well if you didn't purchase said vehicle in which the debt collectors are calling about, then who did? And why are they calling you?

They are calling me because my husband, at that time, had purchased the vehicle as if he was me. Yes, my husband stole my identity. Isn't that crazy? Well, it's true. It really happened. He purchased an entire car in my name, and I was not present. I just told you that I never graced the dealership in which it was purchased. Trust me, it was a significant breach of trust between a husband and wife. It was betrayal at its finest!

Those several months soon turned into four long years. This process allowed me to go through the pressing as I attempted to explain to the lender that this debt was not mine to pay. Do you think the bank cared about my sob story? All they knew was that they had a purchase agreement signed by me for a BMW. They were not concerned one bit about how my name appeared there, and I struggled through this misappropriation of debt.

Four years!

During that season, God pressed and crushed me. He was grinding, and He was teaching. He taught me how to stay in His presence during testing and trials. He taught me how to pray even when it seemed that nothing was happening. He taught me how to trust Him regardless of the circumstances. Finally, He taught me how to worship during struggle.

Anyone can worship when the sun is shining but what about when the rain comes? For me, this seemed like four years of rain.

I tried to negotiate this debt away. It destroyed my credit so if I hoped to purchase anything in the future, or at least for the next seven years, requiring a decent credit score, I probably couldn't count on it. It just would not go away, and I certainly did not have the money to pay the debt. It was like a dark cloud that followed me around by day and night (because I lost a lot of good sleep over this).

I even sought counsel from my Pastor about what steps I could take to rectify this situation. The debt was not mine. Was anyone listening at this point? He suggested that I may just have to "eat it" or just grin and bear it at least for the next seven years. How could this be? I labored before the Lord many nights, out of desperation, seeking a way of escape. I pleaded to the Lord to deliver me out of this debacle.

And then, one day… God answered!

After I had suffered a while, He answered!
After I had been pressed a while, He gave instruction!
After I had been tested a while, He spoke direction!

It was time to release the fragrance of my oil… the oil from my alabaster box. The lender was bought out, and the debt was sold to a new financial institution. God had opened the ears of someone new to hear, and I explained my situation to the representative at the new company (over the phone), who then gave me clear instructions on how to submit an affidavit of identity fraud.

I was nervous, but what did I have to lose at this point?

Following their instructions, I submitted the paperwork. This kicked off a formal investigation. The Lord had spoken. It was about time to release the sweet fragrance of the oil that I had stored in my alabaster box for all these years. And then... I received a letter that read something like this:

> *Congratulations, the investigation is complete, and our findings confirm that you were not present when the vehicle was purchased, and therefore, you are no longer responsible for the debt. The debt has been removed from all three credit reports. You should see this change reflected within 30 days.*

It was the pressing that released the oil and erased the debt! The oil erased it! I share this testimony to tell you to embrace the pressing! As Galatians 5:22 admonishes us, longsuffering is a way of life for the Believer. It is one of the fruits of our walking in the spirit versus our flesh.

It is this longsuffering that increases our faith and builds our trust in the Lord. For "the Lord is not slack concerning His promise, as some men count slackness; but is longsuffering to us-ward, not willing that any should perish, but that all should come to repentance" (2 Peter 3:9).

Sima Clark-Torian, Certified Life and Relationship Coach, Singles' Strategist, Author and Motivational Speaker, is the CEO and founder of *Butterfly Moments with Sima, LLC.*, where her life's purpose is to equip all women with the life skills to cultivate healthy relationships with themselves as well as with others by focusing on building a positive self-image. Sima intends to meet every woman right where she is while encouraging her to establish dynamic yet reasonable goals which will ultimately perpetuate a renewed self-awareness.

Sima believes that it is her self-awareness that attracts functional relationships to her life over relationships that leave her feeling worthless, hopeless, lonely and abandoned.

Sima brings together her degree in Psychology from the University of Virginia, a Coaching Certification by TGCCP, LLC (Mr. Tony Gaskins Jr Certified Coaching Program) and a harvest of painful yet purposeful life experiences, with the intention of changing the world, one beautiful woman at a time. Sima currently resides in Kernersville, NC where she is living life and building a legacy for her two handsome boys, Jeremiah and Jacoby.

Contact her at:
Facebook: Sima Clark Torian
Twitter: @simaytina
Website: www.butterflymomentswithsima.com

CHILDREN ARE A GIFT FROM GOD; YEAH RIGHT!
LADY RHONA AMAYSING

I cannot believe how free and healthy I am! No longer am I ashamed or embarrassed by my story, childhood, adulthood, parenting, drunkenness, promiscuity, idolatry, or infidelities.

The effects of all that shame buried deep down inside led me to live a poverty lifestyle and drove me to obesity. The shame of failure because my grandmother and her husband raised me and that weighed on me.

It weighed on me because when I was a baby, my Dad took me to raise me, but then left me with some strange woman, and called my Mom to come get me. It weighed on me because my Mom turned over her responsibility of me to her Mom. And I felt abandoned, so I clung to people instead of God.

This illegal clinging led to being divorced twice and having three handsome, loveable, and intelligent sons out of wedlock making me a teenage Mom. And I cannot believe I freely and unashamedly admit my life isn't perfect because the pursuit of perfection led to this shame. And now I'm free!

It has been a challenge still to get others' opinions of me as a Mom out of my head. I have to remember that people didn't give me the assignment, God did. I'm neither a perfect person nor a perfect mom. In fact, there are no perfect people. I've done the best I know for my sons.

My ways are not your ways nor are they God's ways at times. We are different people with different gifts, abilities, experiences, and expertise. People's parenting styles vary. For instance, dads parent differently than moms, sisters differently than sisters, and grandparents differently than the parents. No one is wrong unless abuse occurs, of course, it's just different. God made it that way.

The Word says that Children are a gift from God and I have not always felt this way as a Mom; because I was always running, like I was preparing for a marathon, from situation to situation. When I was a child, I ran to my Mom.

Why? Because I was being raised by very strict grandparents.

However, when Mom wouldn't let me stay the one time I ran away to live with her, I began running away by the bus to downtown. I spent hours and hours walking around the dying heart of the city talking to God; and probably looked like a crazy runaway, walking around talking to myself. I prayed for my city to revitalize.

I asked why I had to live with my grandparents, why my Mom didn't want me. I felt as dead as the downtown I walked around. We were both alive once, me and the city.

As the city died, so did I. We were both abandoned! I just became rebellious, so out of line, that my grandparents would be happy to send me to my Mom. Finally, it happened, one day when I was 16, I could go live with Mom, and I was so happy... so excited, and I felt so loved. I eventually even got my own room! YES!

And the thrill was gone with the realization of the mistake I made after a while. Food was sparse! I began eating junk food. I even had to walk home from school. At my grandparents, I barely ate cake that my grandmother baked. Junk food for me at that time was eating fresh fruit. And I was always picked up from school by my grandfather, who sometimes waited hours for me because I would be skipping school.

I was so free at my Mom's, and I mostly loved it. Living with her left me with a lot of free time. To fill the time, I started dating more. I chose a boy from whom I liked before. We began an intimate relationship, and I got pregnant. Pregnant at the age of 16! That did not go over well with anyone including me.

Honestly, we tried all the options. I was too far along to do anything except keep the baby or put it up for adoption when he or she was born. I had dreams for when I graduated from high school. I wanted to be a teacher, fashion model, and actress and I had my eye on California! The University of

California Riverside to be exact. I was so excited about the idea. But becoming a teenage Mom killed that dream.

Additionally, people advised me not to go since I was having a baby. How would I manage and who would watch my child in a strange land where I knew no one my Mom asked? I reluctantly agreed. I started hating being pregnant and saw how this would ruin my life. But then he was born, and he was so cute and beautiful.

And yet, I didn't feel blessed. I suffered from postpartum depression and did all I could to avoid being a Mom. Eventually, I began embracing the reality of motherhood and every day I fed, bathed, clothed and cuddled my son; I was graced for this.

The Beginning of My Decision

One night, after my children were older, the stress of being a parent got to me. I was overwhelmed because we had just gotten evicted, were coming out of homelessness for the first time ever, and I wondered how my eldest son and I, who had just gone off to college in Hawaii, were going to eat! On top of that, my six-year-old son was using the bathroom in his room in the middle of the night and hiding it. This was too much. His disobedience and sneakiness were just profound. And I was fed up.

It was so much that I expressed it to his paternal grandmother and she offered to take him in anytime I needed a break. That offer was soon withdrawn because I almost killed my son that same night, and I needed him to be out of my presence before I went through this felonious first-degree murder.

No one knows this story but now they will. It is the one aspect of being an alcoholic-minded individual that haunts me. It haunted me so badly that I chose not to discipline him physically ever when we did live together again. I did not want to ever get to that point again. And I didn't until a Godly intervention gave me an acceptable way to physically discipline also giving me a renewed sense of self-control.

The night I lost my mind for a few seconds was when I picked my little boy up by the neck, slid him up the wall and began choking the life out of him. Everything went dark in me, and I intently focused on ending his life to stop the hell I was in and that I felt that he was putting me through as well. At this point, I was not saved, but God's still small voice said, "Stop, what are you doing!"

As I type this, I can almost feel Abraham's pain, focus, and saving grace moment when he was ready to kill his son Isaac to prove his faithfulness; and God's voice stopped him in his tracks (Gen 22:11). I suppose I was about to fulfill my allegiance to Satan by killing my son. Consequently, I am always crying and apologizing to my son for this incident. We talked about it entirely when he was about ten, and I don't know if he's fully forgiven me for it, even though he said he has.

I forgave myself for it, too.

The memory of this incident still comes up to try and condemn me, but I know there is no condemnation in God (Rom. 8:1) and my sins are forgiven by God (Isa 43:25). Despite our tumultuous past, my son and God still love me. And for that I am grateful!

The Day I Gave Up!

I sent my son to his grandmother and gave up on parenting for a few years while I got myself together. By this time, I had moved to California (around 1993) and mistakenly begged an old flame to live with me. Every time we fought, I pulled out my Bible to read and encourage myself. I was full of confusion, unhappiness, and even self-hate. Yet, we still got engaged.

I asked my fiancé how much he loved me, and he stood in front of me with arms outstretched and said, *"I love you THIS MUCH!"* I smiled and was still unsure and confused. It didn't make sense until the day I gave my life to Christ.

The Decision

Eventually, my fiancé and I broke up. I was totally broken because a man I knew and loved since high school had referred to what I had given him and me as "SHIT!"

Yes, he said it. When he walked out, I said, "You left your key on the table." He replied, "I don't want that shit." And I supported that decision. I didn't let him back in when he came back banging on the door. I called the police, packed a bag, and went to Arizona to be with family to get away and figure out my next step.

There, I reached out to a Facebook friend because I wanted a hangout and drinking buddy and the woman said, "I don't hang out, but you can come to Bible study." "WHAT!?" "Oh no! I just broke up and moved six hours away, and I want to drown my sorrows and party like it's no tomorrow! And you said let's go to church?" I desperately needed a new friend. So, I decided to go, because I needed a change.

That night, the pastor described my entire last few months as if he was there. What? Who told you what I was doing and how I was living, sir!? And after Bible study, she invited me back for Easter service. I wasn't sure because the Bible study was salt to the open wound of my heart and life. It didn't help that I ran into another ex from Detroit that week who had become a pastor in Arizona! WOW. Really God? You are really piling on the evidence of change.

So, Easter Sunday, that Facebook friend came and picked me up for church. And then it happened... *The altar call.* The pastor put up a picture and an internal conversation began. It was a picture of Jesus with his arms outstretched. And I immediately thought about my ex who just left me who claimed to have loved me THIS much.

Jesus said, "He said he loved you THIS much. No. I love you THIS much!" I was like, "Wow, he didn't love me THIS much because he left me." "But I drink. And when I come to the altar I don't want to drink anymore. If I come to the altar can I have one last drink? Can I get drunk today, and it'll be my last. I promise." Jesus said, "Come." So, we were in agreement, and I gave up, I gave up my life, my way, my rights, my plans, my selfishness, my addiction. I accepted Jesus that Easter 2011 and a weight lifted.

And I did go home that evening, went to the liquor store and bought a fifth of Martell. I drank and drank and enjoyed that Martell and drank until half of the bottle was gone. I had it in a rocks glass. *Martell on the rocks. I didn't drink cheap*! And at about 3 a.m. bar time that was it! At that moment, I no longer had a desire or taste for alcoholic beverages. I was done forever with drinking after 16 years! So, I have been sober for seven years now. Many days, it's a challenge to figure out what to do now that I don't drink and party anymore.

I often don't go to friends' parties because I do not want to be around drinking and the temptation to drink. Because they often forget and offer me a drink or ask me to pass a drink or clean up and I don't even touch it, not even the empties. And empty beer bottles and cans are worth 10 cents apiece in Michigan!

Redemption Confirmed with Delayed Dreams Realized

Not long after the day that I gave myself up to Christ, the pastor of the church called for a quiet time with God. "Go home; be quiet and ask God what He wants you to do," he said.

So, I did. And I was not disappointed. God answered my question quickly. He said," To teach people to read." I responded, "Ok. But why do you want people to read?" He said, "So they can read the Bible." Me, "Oh ok, cool." I wondered what people and I landed in children's ministry and stayed, so I got my answer.

Ever since He gave me my purpose, I've been "working out the vision," as Pastor Moore said. For example, I tried tutoring ESL adults to read English through Mesa Literacy. Then, I tried getting my master's for teaching credentials online at Grand Canyon University using a scholarship; I had 3.0 GPA but got kicked out because being a Mom came 1st, and I had to focus on my son's health and education.

Eventually, we homeschooled for three years successfully. At the same time, I was accepted to Virginia Union University's Weekend school for teaching licensure.

During that time, I also volunteered in the Children's ministry at Liberation. And again, I asked God for more information about my assignment; asking Him why he wanted people to read the Bible. He referred me to the Bible, Ephesians 4:12, "to equip the saints for the work of the ministry, for building up the body of Christ."

To fulfill the childhood dream of modeling, I went to a curvy, plus-sized modeling call. However, I didn't grow to be tall. I am petite and plus-sized. I thought my dream was impossible. And yet, I was selected to rip the runway. I finally understand what being "Graced for this" means! I was riding past a school bus lot and saw a hiring sign and said to myself, "well maybe I can be a bus driver." And Holy Spirit said, "You're NOT graced for that." Well, what am I graced for? "You know already."

For me, that's teaching. Some things you cannot do because GOD didn't give that to you. I was graced for the Detroit Free Press International Marathon, all 26.2 miles, but because I DIDN'T prepare, my body and the anointing ran out halfway. I was calling on Jesus in Canada around mile 5!

Trust me, I asked God if I were to continue and he said: "I DIDN'T send you out here to ride the bus. Finish."

I finished 13.1 miles instead!

You too are graced to make a hard thing look easy. The anointing will keep you going in the hard thing. But, if you didn't prepare to go ALL the way, then FINISH what you start, where you can.

My mantras: #BeAFinisher #SheDidWhatSheCould #InternationalMarathoner

Rhona "Amaysing" Mays Foote is fun-loving, stay at home mom who lives in Detroit, Michigan. She is an inspirational powerhouse model, writer and now Best-Selling Author who gives 100% to anything she endeavors to do.

Rhona was published in The Metro Times where she interned while studying health administration and journalism at Central Michigan University. Raised by her grandparents and certainly no stranger to life's share of experiences, Rhona has overcome numerous obstacles, including pregnancy at age 16 and suffering homelessness at age 36 while raising two children of her three children.

Through marriage and divorce, alcoholism and sobriety, Rhona has demonstrated the strength of a true diamond. Refusing to accept no for an answer, Rhona encourages many and will embrace any challenge she faces with strength and courage. Rhona has triumphed over abandonment, rejection, shame, perfection, and many other hurdles.

One of her greatest achievements, aside from being in sobriety for seven years, is accepting Christ as Savior. She attributes all to Him and lives to share His love with others.

Teaching is her passion, and she shares this gift as a Substitute Teacher in Detroit. She is truly an AMAYSING woman.

Contact her at:
Facebook: Rhona Amaysing
Email: Rhonaamaysing@gmail.com

BROKEN BUT MENDING
LADY TIESHA C. FRONTIS

What is an Alabaster Box?

The Bible speaks of two alabaster box incidents. Both involve women; one of whom was Mary of Bethany, who brought ointment in the box to anoint Jesus.

The Greek word translated "alabaster box" in the KJV, as well as "flask," "jar" and "vial" in other translations, is alabastron, which can also mean "perfume vase." Alabaster was a stone commonly located in Israel. It was a hard stone resembling white marble and was one of the precious stones used in the decoration of Solomon's Temple (1 Chronicles 29:2).

So, the container the two women used to carry the perfumed oil was constructed of a white, marble-like substance. In biblical times, people placed ointment, oils, and perfumes in vessels made of alabaster, which kept them pure and unspoiled. The boxes were often sealed or made fast with wax, to prevent the perfume from escaping. In the story we see when Mary broke open her alabaster box, "the house was filled with the fragrance of the perfume" (John 12:3).

Alabaster was a durable enough substance to keep the oil or perfume completely sealed until the time of its use. This leads me to share with you how my Alabaster box helped me move from brokenness to being mended.

What's in my Alabaster box? God showed me my Alabaster box consists of the wall cavities of my heart. It holds the most precious vital part of life that I need to live yet it also contains the most painful residue of my brokenness. My Alabaster box eventually became a lifeline for me during some of the roughest times in my life. The experiences I am speaking of today are that of surviving homelessness, divorce and the loss of my children in a custody battle.

After separating from my ex-husband, I found myself and our three children living in a hotel. I never intended for my marriage to fail, but the reality is, I married out of season.

What I mean by out of season is that I didn't seek God's direction on my marriage. I married because I grew up without my father in my life and I had vowed that my children would not grow up without theirs. When I became pregnant with our first son, I lived up to the vow I made to myself, yet God was not in that decision. Through dealing with the divorce, I turned away from God wholeheartedly and began to self-medicate the world's way. I didn't become a drug addict or an alcoholic, but instead, depression and anxiety became prevalent in my daily life. I was what I refer to as a functioning "Depressivict."

Being a "Depressivict," 90% of the time I was confined to my bed, dark rooms, crying excessively, very moody, fatigued, lost interest in life, slowly pulled away from the church, and had frequent panic attacks. I started partying and depending on the comfort of men to fill the voids or emptiness in my heart. Everything that looks good and comes easy more than likely is not good for you.

Being an entrepreneur at heart, I owned a thrift store, a café, and worked full-time, which required me to travel almost weekly. Due to me functioning as a "Depressivict." I did not recognize the enemy's' trap. Those decisions, later on, cost me to lose my children in a custody battle with my ex-husband and as a result, also caused me to close my businesses.

It didn't make sense to me. I thought I was providing for my children and me. When the judge ruled in my ex-husband's favor, I thought my life was over, and I was ready to "code." This meant not being able to wake up every morning and hear their voices or take them to football and cheerleading practices. No more breaking up sibling rivalries.

I was distraught. The wall cavities of my heart felt like they were broken beyond repair. I didn't want to eat, breathe or live at times. Prayer, what was that? I had no desire to pray, no desire to praise, no desire to worship, man I didn't even want to do church.

So, I didn't.

I truly battled with depression. Silent Spiritual Killers slowly invaded my mind and body causing me to experience a spiritual death on the inside. My heart kept trying to pump the necessary elements through my body, but I was numb... spiritually dead.

The Resuscitation:

Separation to being homeless to getting a divorce to becoming childless left me pondering some questions such as: What did I do God to deserve this? Why me, I am a good mom? How much more can I take? I have lost it all, why am I still here?

Can you say, *"But God?"*

The turning point in my life was seeing how hard it was for my children to be away from their mom. I had to put my feelings aside, realize that they are human and that this was hard for them too. Being uprooted from the only life and home they knew was very devastating for them. I knew I had to be there for my babies, but more importantly, God reminded me that this was much bigger than me.

God instructed me that there was some mending and healing that needed to take place in my own life. I couldn't understand at the time, but eventually, I saw why I had to endure those trials in my life. When there is a calling on your life, and your love for God outweighs your hardships, there is hope. Hope for you to live again and be restored. My love for God allowed reparation to occur within the wall cavities of my heart.

You see, the heart is a powerful muscle. Research shows that the human heart muscle cells can regenerate after a heart attack.

Although I didn't experience an actual heart attack, my heart was attacked by traumatic experiences. Only God could mend the brokenness in my heart. Many prayed for me, spoke into my life, and even provided counseling. Nothing others did seemed to be enough. During this process, I had to dig deep, re-activate my Faith, do the work and REST in God for Him to begin to take me from broken to mending. Let me share these things that assisted me in my process:

1. *Recognize the silent Spiritual Killers killing me and causing me to experience a spiritual death (i.e., bitterness, self-pity, rejection, depression, disobedience, slothfulness, pride, isolation and spiritual starvation to name a few).* "The thief comes only to steal and kill and destroy; I have come that they may have life, and have it to the full." (John 10:10 NIV)

2. *Empty myself of all guilty and negative thoughts that were blocking me from God's promises.* "Are you tired? Worn out? Burned out on religion? Come to me. Get away with me, and you'll recover your life. I'll show you how to take a real rest. Walk with me and work with me—watch how I do it. Learn the unforced rhythms of grace. I won't lay anything heavy or ill-fitting on you. Keep company with me, and you'll learn to live freely and lightly." (Matthew 11:28-29 MSG)

3. *Sit at the feet of Jesus and honor Him with my praise, worship, and prayers.* "Shout with joy to the Lord, all the earth! Worship the Lord with gladness. Come before him, singing with joy. Acknowledge that the Lord is God! He made us, and we are his. We are his people, the sheep of his pasture. Enter his gates with thanksgiving; go into his courts with praise. Give thanks to him and praise his name. For the Lord is good, His unfailing love continues forever, and his faithfulness continues to each generation." (Psalms 100 NLT)

"And he said to them, "This kind cannot be driven out by anything but prayer." (Mark 9:29 ESV)

4. *Tell my testimony to other women who were going through the same trials I had encountered.* "And they have defeated him by the blood of the Lamb and by their testimony. And they did not love their lives so much that they were afraid to die." (Revelation 12:11 NLT)

You may ask why I say *mending*. I say that because healing is an ongoing process. We may be healed in one area of life but if we step out of the will of God, that area may get affected again and may even seep over to another area of your life.

Let's examine the story of The Potter and the Clay in Jeremiah 18: 1-10 MSG God told Jeremiah, "Up on your feet! Go to the potter's house. When you get there, I'll tell you what I have to say." So, I went to the potter's house, and sure enough, the potter was there, working away at his wheel. Whenever the pot the potter was working on turned out badly, as sometimes happens when you are working with clay, the potter would simply start over and use the same clay to make another pot.

Then, God's message came to me:

> "Can't I do just as this potter does, people of Israel?" God's Decree! "Watch this potter. In the same way that this potter works his clay, I work on you, people of Israel. At any moment I may decide to pull up a people or a country by the roots and get rid of them. But if they repent of their wicked lives, I will think twice and start over with them. At another time I might decide to plant a people or country, but if they don't cooperate and won't listen to me, I will think again and give up on the plans I had for them."

Little by little, I began to feel air passing through my lungs. I could feel the warmth of the blood running through my veins. My heartbeat started to have a rhythm again. My Alabaster box began to heal. Praise and Worship were my ointments: oils and perfumes I learned to use were put in vessels made of alabaster (stonewalls of my heart), keeping them pure and unspoiled.

My heart was durable enough to withstand the pain, the brokenness, and the hardships that I had to endure. When the seal of my Alabaster box was opened, I released a sound that was pleasing to God.

Through my Praise and Worship, I was able to make it through those challenging moments in my life. I honored God through Praise and Worship. I anointed his feet with my thanksgiving; He allowed me to go through homelessness, marriage, separation, divorce and losing my children all while finding my Purpose, where my total "Me" meets "My Destiny" as the Founder/ CEO of Know Your Self-Worth Ministries, Inc.

My friend, never underestimate the hand of God. He will never take you to a place that you are not equipped to go, nor will he lead you to a place that is not part of your Destiny; a place meant to grow and develop you. He led me through the valley, and there were times I wanted to give up. I didn't want to praise. I didn't want to worship. I didn't want to pray and seek His face, but I learned in the valley experience how to LIVE.

I learned what God intended for me during this season. I had to discipline myself to intercede daily and continue to nurture my relationship with Him through the reading of His Word, fasting, and Praise and Worship.

Allowing myself to go through the process was not easy, but it was worth it. I am here to tell you that at times it will get hard but giving up is not an option. You are strong and will overcome. I pray that through my testimony your life will forever be changed.

Tiesha C. Frontis is the founder and CEO of ***Know Your Self Worth, Inc.*** This organization, birthed in 2013, was created to inspire, uplift and teach women how God sees them and how they should see themselves through Him. She is a native of Charlotte, N.C., but relocated to Durham, NC in 1993 to pursue her college education at North Carolina Central University, where she graduated with a dual Bachelor's Degree in Chemistry and Biology.

She believes education is important and is currently pursuing a dual Master's Degree at Pfeiffer College and will also pursue her Doctorate in Theology. She wholeheartedly believes in her movement... *Know Your Self-Worth.* She is a woman of purpose, faith, and virtue, having persevered through diverse challenges including molestation, promiscuity, addiction, domestic abuse, miscarriage, homelessness, divorce and so much more.

Tiesha lives to share her story with other women and men, encouraging them that they can make it and they can survive. She is a true testimony of resilience and triumph.

Contact her at:
Twitter: www.twitter.com/kyswnetwork
Instagram: www.instagram.com/tieshacoomahsafrontis
Facebook: tieshacfrontisknowyourselfworth
Website: www.knowyourselfworth.org
Email: knowyourselfworth@gmail.com

I AM HEALED
LADY CHRISTINA CLEMONTS

"I can't feel my feet."

I seriously cannot feel my feet... Like I slept with my feet under me all night, and they fell asleep or something.

Only I didn't fall asleep like that. And no matter how hard I try to shake off the numbness, I still can't feel them. They won't wake up! Perhaps I haven't awakened yet. Maybe I'm dreaming? This was the start of a nightmare that neither I nor my feet could seem to awaken from.

I spent the next 11 months going to doctors, neurologists, getting blood work, MRIs, and a spinal tap only to hear the words, *"I'm sorry. You have MS."*

According to the National Multiple Sclerosis Society, "MS is an unpredictable, often disabling disease of the central nervous system that disrupts the flow of information within the brain, and between the brain and body there is a protective coat around our spinal cords called the myelin sheath. Sclerosis literally means 'scars.'"[1]

Imagine an electrical wire. You plug it in and whatever you plug in, works; a light, a radio, etc. One day, you look and see that the protective coating around the cord is breaking down and exposing wire, you plug it in, and you find that there may be a short in the lamp or radio. Lights flicker, and the radio goes in and out. That is what happens when a scar forms or the myelin sheath breaks down. It's like a short circuit occurs in the body of a person who suffers from MS.

Some people experience numbness in multiple areas of their body such as cognitive issues, bladder problems, spasms, and much more. Each person may have a different experience.

I was 26 years old, just had my third child… a girl. I was a young, active mommy; and I had all these plans. My then live-in boyfriend and father of my daughter tried to understand what I felt—but could not. He'd get me to soak my feet, take me to the ER, yet nothing helped.

My words and thoughts, "I don't have time for this. I have too much to do. God, are you punishing me? Is it because I am not living right? I stopped serving you? I don't go to church anymore?

What did I do Lord?"

---

[1] National Multiple Sclerosis Society, https://www.nationalmssociety.org/What-is-MS

At the time, I couldn't answer those questions. All I knew was that I could no longer feel my feet and my balance was off. I fell often and grew tired after simple tasks. And that's not all; the numbness was now in my legs and chest. Even wearing a bra hurt.

The diagnoses came in December of 2001, a week or two before Christmas, and like the signal from the electrical cord to the lamp, my life as I knew it was totally interrupted.

What would my future hold? Would I need a wheelchair? Will I end up in a nursing home being spoon fed and bedridden like some of the patients I'd taken care of as a CNA at that time? I got so wrapped up in my carnal thoughts and all the whys, I forgot to go to the source, the only one who could answer these haunting questions. I forgot there was a healer, a God that raised the dead. Surely, He was the same God; He'll do it for me, right? My thought process was unstable, and I would wrestle with my thoughts in relation to God's truth. That state of mind led me to a period in which I thought I would surely die.

In all my questioning, in all my "woe is me, why me and how" life still had a way of moving on. Even if you don't want to, life does, and it will. My bills still needed to be paid; my kids needed to eat. Life continued. And, life didn't wait for me to process all of this information.

In the midst of everything, my boyfriend left, and I had to find another place to live for my three kids and me.

Thank God for my sister. She welcomed us in for a couple of months until finally, I was able to get a small two-bedroom apartment; independent and on my own again.

Life.

So here I am, single mom to three kids. Single parenting is hard enough. Throw in sickness and boy, oh boy! Let's just say I had to hustle as much as I could while balancing mommy-hood and trying to have a life. I worked as a CNA full time before being diagnosed. It was money, but it took a toll on my body once I started feeling sick.

Previously, when I lost the feeling in my feet, I had consulted with a few nurses, yet they had way too many opinions as to what it could be. *My God.* Finally, I told them about the MS, then everyone said, "We thought it might be that, but didn't want to tell you."

Though it was tough, I had favor on my job. I would get assigned "watches" or one on ones; which means I had to sit with one patient instead of having several. That was a lot easier depending on the patient. Some were elderly, and if you ever tried to calm an elderly patient who has Dementia or Alzheimer's, you know that they may look weak, but honey they can have the strength of 2-3 people!

Although I was working, and getting some child support, money was still short for rent and bills. Even with rental assistance, I couldn't make ends meet. Looking back, I didn't know how to budget which is another story that deserves a chapter of its own. I was overwhelmed! Three kids, three different fathers; not because I was promiscuous, but because I looked for love in all the wrong places. That is also a different testimony for a different time.

So overwhelmed, bills underpaid, and the rent due.

I began keeping to myself. I would take the kids to daycare, and if I was off work, I'd go home and sleep my day away. I would get up, pick my children up and just go through the rest of my day. The lights were on, but no one was home.

Thoughts of taking my own life crept into my head. Then I'd shake it off. Then they would creep back in. You see, when you are in a place of instability, you are all over the place! I didn't have the mind of Christ, so I could not capture those thoughts that exalted themselves above Christ. The enemy told me I was unworthy, ugly, and sick. He told me I wasn't a good mom. "Look at you!" he'd say. "You can't take care of your kids. Let your sister have them. She can do a better job than you! You're so worthless!" I believed the lies. If you haven't made Christ your firm foundation, you will believe every lie the enemy throws at you.

Eventually, believing the lies so much, I gave into them. It was a slow downward fall. Depression doesn't just happen one day. You do not wake up and say, "Hey, today will be a great day to take my life." No, you contemplate it slowly. You think about it every day; it consumes you. You start to wonder how you'll do it, or how it will be after the fact. I cried out for help silently.

Subtlety.

One evening I finally felt it was time. I had a reckless evening. I was trying to "hook up" with a guy friend after an evening of dancing and drinking. I was craving attention; any kind of attention and of course, a man was my drug of choice. I sought out comfort, but he was suddenly unavailable. I called, and he wouldn't pick up. Just as I got home, his number popped up. Only it wasn't him. It was a young lady who made sure I knew just why he wasn't available.

That was the straw that broke the camel's back! The enemy whispered, "No one wants you. You're horrible, do it now." He reminded me that I had a bottle of sleeping pills. "Write a letter to your family." *Oh, my God. Am I really doing this?* I thought.

Yes, I decided. No one needs you. Die. Just die.

So, I wrote the letter, laid on the couch, took the pills and closed my eyes. Suddenly, clear as day, I heard a sweet soft voice, "Your daughter's birthday is in a few days, do you want her to remember this day every year for the rest of your life? Get up, call your friend and go to the hospital."

That is what I did. I called my friend, and she called my mom. My mom came and picked up my babies, and I went to the hospital. I went to get rest and help; spending four days "away" to sort everything out. There I was diagnosed with depression, given anti-depression pills, and told to see a professional.

Her name was Molly. I liked her right away. She was an unbiased ear; she listened, and I talked.

Allow me to take a moment to say this: the devil is the Father of lies. His main mission before his time is up is to kill, steal, and destroy YOU! *Yes... you my friend.* You may say, "Well who am I?" *You are the child of a King. You have a purpose! You are chosen.* The enemy knew when I was being formed in my mother's womb that I was here to help set folks free! So, his job is to stop us! Oh, but what a mighty God we serve! Let me encourage you, to know and recognize the symptoms of depression, and please get help. It's okay to get help.

The next several years flew by, and I went to school to become an IT Professional (I'm still doing that, thank God)! Then, just as I thought I was getting a grasp on everything, another illness struck my body.

Can two autoimmune diseases live in one body? I found out that they indeed can. Contracting a lung infection, I landed in the ER. The doctor came in to say that my kidney levels were high, and I should have it checked out ASAP.

I went to my doctor, who was a nephrologist or kidney doctor. In August 2014, after an ultrasound and biopsy, it was determined that I had Lupus nephritis. I got in my car took a deep breath and let out a scream, *"THIS IS NOT FAIR! WHY LORD! WHY?!"*

I was so angry, angry at God, myself... just angry. I called my sister, she talked me down from the ledge, and I pulled myself together. "It's going to be OK," I said to myself. "You are not going down like this."

If I learned anything, it was that God is faithful and He allowed me to go through it, so that I could be a testimony to someone else! My friends, over 2000 years ago, Jesus gave his life for us. He took those stripes for us. I am a witness that His love for us kept him on that cross. Those stripes represent MS; they represent Lupus, Cancer, diabetes—you name it. He took those stripes for me. He took them for you.

I have a beautiful family. I'm so glad I didn't let the enemy win. I thank God for my mom, who never judged me and just loved me. My sister was my rock, and my children are my heartbeats. I have some really good friends who've been with me from day one and a church family who prays constantly!

Today, I am stable; my kidneys are now functioning almost normally. I haven't had a relapse with the MS in nearly four years. I speak life! I shall live and not die and declare the Lord's works! I am confident in this one thing, that no matter what it feels like, He sent His word and He healed me... present tense.

I stand in my truth, and my truth is that *by His stripes I am healed.* For this I worship Him.

Christina E. Clemonts is a spunky, inspirational "girl" who was born in Germany because her father was in the military. Christina is the epitome of resilience, as she too has faced numerous obstacles and overcome them with grace.

After her parents divorced, she lived with her mother and sister. Life dealt her many blows, and there were times she wanted to give up; however, God's love overcame the challenges she faced. Diagnosed with Multiple Sclerosis (MS) in 2001 and Lupus Nephritis in 2014, depression, attempted suicide, homelessness, and financial hardship came knocking at her door while raising her children.

Searching for love in all the wrong places, Christina found herself broken and empty which ultimately led her to accept Christ to heal the wounded places in her heart and soul. These challenges propelled her to minister to others about God's healing power in her life. She now empowers other women around the world through her ministry #IAMHEALED and her Blog Talk Radio show by the same name.

Currently, she resides in New Jersey with her teenage daughter. She has two adult children (son and daughter) and four handsome grandsons.

Alabaster Box is her first publication.

TRAUMA TRINKETS TURNED TO WORSHIP TREASURE
MINISTER ELAINE MONTFORD

Matthew 26: 6-12 tells a very familiar story of the woman, Mary, who poured precious, costly perfume from her alabaster jar anointing Jesus' head. There were murmurings of disapproval from others in attendance at her very presence; and when the disciples witnessed what she had done, they scolded her for what they perceived as a waste.

Jesus alone was completely aware of the significance of her offering, and He immediately came to her rescue and defense.

I love the song by Cece Winans that so beautifully shares this story as if the woman herself was narrating it. It paints a lyrical panoramic account that allows the listener to gain an intimate view of Mary, and it even gives us a transparent and vulnerable picture of her emotional struggle as she described the denigrating remarks others whispered about her.

What I love most about this story is her liberating, [victorious] deliverance from the prying eyes, judgmental whispers, and the rejection by others, through the love and acceptance of Jesus for her, and her gift! My heart is filled with compassion for this precious sister every time I hear this song, and each time I study the account as recorded in the Bible.

Delivered from a similar place after suffering many things due to the cruelty or misconception of others, I dealt with a personal battle with some manner of sickness and disease for many years that only seemed to add to my perceived lack of value, and I can readily identify with the pain and anguish she must have suffered. After enduring all of these issues, I came to better understand the cost of that precious oil in Mary's alabaster box… or of equal importance to me, and to this testimony, the cost of the oil in my own alabaster box.

I grew up in the Church, so there was a strong religious foundation in place for me from early on. But for many years, I wrestled with the true legitimacy of this love, forgiveness, and salvation that I'd heard preached and taught about for most of my life. No matter how I tried, I could not convince myself of this great gift being available to everyone; especially to me.

My skepticism rested on my confusion about what love looked and felt like from an early age. I was confident that what I experienced from my parents was love; but some of the atrocities I suffered at the hands of others that came initially under the guise of love, caused me to pull away from anyone who was not my parent or a sparse number of trusted family.

As I grew, and these types of incidents/assaults kept occurring, I shut myself away in an emotional shell. I didn't want to keep hurting or being hurt anymore. Also, I began to inwardly resent my parents for not protecting me from these offenses that they were not even aware existed.

In essence, as the years progressed, I tried to be good enough so that people would stop hurting me; and if that didn't work, maybe I could be quiet enough so that no one would even notice that I was alive.

I needed desperately to be rescued; saved from this living hell. I wanted more than anything for God to love me and save me; so I tried to be good enough to earn God's love.

After being baptized at an early age, I began this quest to "earn" God's affection. Little did I know then, not only was that an impossible task; it was also unnecessary.

Although I had the religion thing down pretty well, I was still millions of miles away from a true relationship with God. I was living in the shallowness of religious actions, which is a far cry from the depth of love, protection, and guidance available by way of a right relationship with Him. For all intents and purposes, I was an expert at "appearing" to know God deeply, but all I had learned was how to go through the motions.

Somewhere deep within me though, I was very aware that there had to be more. So, I kept praying and studying… and searching. I would eventually come to embrace the truth of

Jeremiah 29: 13, "You will seek me and find me when you seek me with all your heart."

My search yielded me the fulfillment I had longed for, and once I understood that I would never be "good" enough to earn God's love, but that I didn't need to be because He offers it freely to all who will receive it —my life changed forever! I began to live in a level of love, peace, and joy I had previously doubted even existed, or that could only exist for others.

My mountaintop euphoria was slightly dampened when I realized that although God had accepted me with all my faults, flaws, and scars. Apparently, the "church folk" had their own standards. So, I set out to try and gain their approval and acceptance. Here I was, living the scene from Cece Winans' song, but nothing I did seemed to satisfy them for very long; either it wasn't enough, or they thought I felt I was better than them!

As much as I love and respect others, I came to appreciate that I did not need their approval or permission to be me! My ultimate victory came when I fully grasped the knowledge that I only needed to live up to God's standard... not man's. Not even those cloaked in religious piousness.

When my mother was alive, people would often say to her that they wanted to be just like her (spiritually) when they grew up. My mother's response was always, "Be careful what you ask for. I'm probably not all that you think I am, and you have no idea what it cost me to become whoever it is that you think I have become." In other words, what I think my mother was saying (and I wholeheartedly concur), *"You don't know the cost of the oil, you don't know the cost of my praise... you don't know the cost of the oil in my alabaster box."*

I am growing to love earnestly and openly, with the true agape love of my Father; so I place no judgments on you or your trinkets because like mine, each of those trinkets came with a hefty cost attached. My mother's proverbial wisdom helped me to see that each of our alabaster boxes is filled with trinkets from years on this journey.

Thanks to that imparted knowledge, I simply smile when I spot the looks of disapproval toward my expression of worship; because I know that those who disapprove cannot possibly comprehend the cost of my praise!

The trinkets in my box may have started out as bitter tears of tests, trials, and disappointments that the Holy Spirit collected and cleansed through the purification process of His love. My trinkets may also have been misconception and rejection that God turned into compassion and forgiveness; or pain and suffering that grew into beautiful flowers of grace and mercy.

Yes, the process of purification took my trinkets of trauma and transformed them into an expensive perfumed oil that releases its sweet-smelling savor through the rendering of my worship.

So, as the song says: *"I've come to pour my praise on Him like oil..."*

Minister Elaine Roundtree Montford is an Author and Poet. She is the author of *The Birth of Victorious Destiny*, a contributing columnist of The Bridge Builder column for The Acts of Women Of Power Magazine, and co-author with best-selling author Elder Desireé Harris-Bonner of the Christian fiction novel series *Love Never Fails* (scheduled for release in 2019).

Additionally, she is a contributing author for the second **TESTIFY** book *Unmerited Favor & Divine Provision* as well as *The Jots & Tittle of Scribes and Storytellers* Anthology.

Minister Montford is a member of the ministerial support team of Hurst Chapel African Methodist Episcopal Church (Winter Haven, FL), and a charter member and past Central FL Region Director for Women Of Power, Inc., founded by Pastor BJ Relefourd.

She is currently working on her second book *Moving Forward in Victorious Destiny*.

Contact her at:
Email: **elaine.montford27@gmail.com**
Facebook: elaineroundtreemontford

THE ROAD LEAST TAKEN
ANGELICA TORRICO WOODBURY

I would like to share a little bit about my background.

Born in Lima, Peru, I came to the United States when I was just around two-years-old, and then raised in College Point Queens, New York.

Growing up, I was surrounded by my grandparents, aunties and uncles, cousins, both parents and my two brothers. We all lived together; my aunt had a big house that she rented as two apartments—one to my grandparents and another to my parents, aunt and uncle, and cousin.

When I entered the school system, I did not speak English, only Spanish. I did not want to learn how to speak English. I remember when I was in Kindergarten my teacher and classmates did not understand me and I did not have many friends, until the second grade when I started to speak a bit more English.

I was attending P.S 129 Q (Public School), and by third grade, I struggled with reading, mathematics, comprehension, writing, spoken language, or reasoning abilities.

Thankfully, I had a teacher who noticed that I had problems and I could not catch up with the rest of the classmates. The teacher called for a meeting with my parents and school psychologist, speech-language pathologist, and physicist to evaluate my learning difficulties. I remember being placed in the room with a lot of different specialists working as a team to perform various testing to evaluate me.

The IEP results came back, and I was diagnosed with a learning disability and a Speech disorder. I was then taken out of P.S. 129Q and placed into P.S 79 because the latter school provided special education classes.

At the age of nine years, this shy little girl could not understand why I was going to another school. *Why was this happening? Why had God had made me this way? Why could I not learn like other kids?*

In the new school, it was hard; I was depressed, and I cried a lot because I did not have many friends to play with or talk to. I was embarrassed that I was not with the normal kids.

During this time, I also gained a lot of weight because I only wanted to sleep and not do anything. I wanted to learn more—feeling that I was being held back and that the teacher did not understand me. It took a little time to fully realize what was going on, but I did my best, and with the help that I received there, I was able to do a bit better on my next evaluation.

In middle school, the work was becoming easier, and I was not being challenged; therefore, they decided to place me in a few mainstream (regular) classes. While there, I continued to press on to prove to them that I could be placed in regular classes permanently. So, by the time I started high school, and following another evaluation, I had finally earned the right to be in a mainstream classroom full time.

Still, at the beginning of my senior year, my school counselor told me that since I had been in special education that I should not think of going into a four-year college… that someone like me would not be able to succeed academically. At that moment, I decided that what my school counselor said could either impact me negatively *or* positively, so I chose to use this life event to challenge myself to develop my career goals by going to a two-year college.

This is where my journey began.

I was interested in working in the medical field in the following areas: medical reception, medical office administrator, billing, coder, medical translator, and assistant. I decided to pursue and continue my education at a four-year college by attending St. Joseph's College where I received my Bachelor of Science in Healthcare Administration with GPA 3.35.

To further my education in the medical field, I went to Molloy College to obtain certifications in coding specialist, and healthcare billing for physicians through their continuing education and professional development division. I also took an interpreter for health and health service training where I completed three levels of interpreter classes.

Additionally, I have a passion to become a mental health counselor, where I can use all my previous knowledge and experience to help children who are going through it.

As I continued on my path, not realizing why all of this happened or its purpose, I tried to hide that painful portion of my journey because I did not want to talk about it. It hurt too much to remember; however, everything came back when my older son, Santiago, was diagnosed with a severe speech disorder when he was three and a half years old. We were told that his learning was at a one-year old's level. As a mother, it brought back memories, and I did not want Santiago to go through what I had gone through.

It broke my heart into little pieces.

I prayed and asked God, "WHY, WHY, WHY Lord? I can't bear this again." I asked God to give me the tools to help Santiago achieve. It was hard work because Santiago did not talk; yet with God, the Speech Therapist, and my husband and me helping him, he scored above average in six months. He was now at a four-year level which made him a normal child.

This is when I truly knew that God had given me a desire to help other children with their learning.

He made me a teacher.

I know that God is not done with me yet; I have a heart to do more and to help other parents. Through ministry and other endeavors, I plan to do just that. My prayers and sincere worship to God are what brought me through... *brought us through.* My husband and I truly love God and want to see others receive the healing for their children that we received for Santiago.

Sharing my story has been difficult, but necessary for my personal growth and for encouraging others. My prayer is that you have been blessed by the words I have shared and that you will continue to seek the Lord for everything you need.

His Word is available to heal.

Angelica Torrico Woodbury is a native of Peru; however, she grew up in College Point, New York. She graduated in 2006 from St. Joseph's College with a Bachelor of Science in Healthcare Administration and is working towards her degree in Public Administration with a concentration in Healthcare Management.

Additionally, she is pursuing an Associate's in Early Childhood Education and Administration from Haywood Community College. Angelica has taught children for the last ten years, as a Substitute teacher, assistant, and co-teacher.

Currently, she is working as a 2nd-grade teacher at a local Christian School. She has achieved much despite many odds that were stacked against her in her younger years. Angelica hopes to obtain her licensure in education and publish her solo book projects soon.

She is married to Minister Jonathan Woodbury and supports her husband in his career as a Licensed Professional Counselor, as well as his endeavors as an Entrepreneur in the travel industry. Together they serve in ministry as pastors and avid community leaders. Angelica and Jonathan have two wonderful boys, Santiago and Joel.

Angelica exclaims, "It has been an amazing journey working with my husband in our non-profit ministry and our travel business."

You can connect with her via Facebook.

THE EXPERIENCE OF A LIFETIME
LADY LETISHA GALLOWAY

It was challenging for me to write about my experience. I wasn't sure how I could relate it to the woman and her alabaster box.

I thought, "Well I don't have an alabaster box." I don't have long hair like the woman, and Jesus is not in human form today, so I couldn't do what she did even if I desired to.

How many of us would consider wiping dry another person's feet with our hands and a towel let alone our hair? I would imagine very few would be willing to wash someone's feet and dry them with the hair on our heads. It takes a significant amount of love and humbleness not to be bothered like the woman with alabaster box.

I found it interesting that her sins were known. I thought about how gossip travels fast. If there were social media back, then her sins would have been known all over Facebook, Twitter, and Instagram, etc.

Sometimes people spread gossip and confuse it as gospel. Nothing good comes from scandal except the potential to ruin another person's reputation. It is clear to me that people spent way too much time in her business and not tending to their affairs. She lived a publicly sinful life. Nothing she did seemed to be a secret.

Instead of worrying about their sinful ways, the people where she lived labeled her. They saw her sins as greater than theirs. They had no regard for a person's feelings. They just wanted to gossip. She was infamous for her sins. She was known for all of her mistakes. She was thought to be evil. The way she lived her life was seen as a disgrace. The telling about this woman and her sins could have been fueled by jealousy. She was a woman with means… she could afford an alabaster box.

Women are notorious for belittling each other because they look at another person's belongings and desire them.

I was different than the woman with the alabaster box. I, like many others, was a woman who thought what I did wouldn't be noticed. I tried to hide in plain sight. And other times I just tried to hide. It seemed the more I tried to hide my sins, the more they became known. Two months after I graduated high school I became pregnant. Much like the woman with the alabaster box I was criticized and talked down to.

People knew that I was unwed and 18 years old having a baby. The first four months of my pregnancy were horrible. I never knew people in my own family could be so cruel. I didn't know people from church could have such a nasty attitude. I knew what I did was wrong. I wasn't ready for the whispers that came along with the sin of fornication. I was unable to hide my sin because each month my stomach grew as there was a precious life inside.

In 2001 things seemed to get worse. There was terrible event after terrible event. The whispers increased. The judgment continued. I believe that people should be corrected but not in a demeaning matter. There were ways that people could have talked to me just as people could have been kinder to the woman with the alabaster box. In 2001 people continued to gossip about me. I was involved with my abuser as a teenager. We broke up. I became pregnant with my son in 2000 by an ex-boyfriend. I wasn't married. I was criticized by the church, and what I call Super Saints or those who walk around as if they have never sinned. I eventually went back to my abuser.

When I was going through domestic violence, people gossiped and said that I was stupid to stay. Some said that I must like being hit. Instead of asking me questions, the news of my being involved in a domestic violence situation spread among those I was closest to or, so I thought.

In May 2001, after my son was 'allegedly' murdered by my abuser, there was no hiding. I lived in a small county where all towns were less than 15 miles apart. The news traveled fast. There was plenty of media coverage through the newspapers, and the murder trial was often on the front page of the paper. People that I had grown up with turned their backs on me. Some of my own family turned their backs on me.

I felt alone and ashamed.

While what my ex-boyfriend was charged with had nothing to do with me I was made to feel as though I had committed the biggest sin of all. I was told that I should have known that if he hit me, he would hurt the baby. I was told that it was my fault.

Some women I had gone to school with said I was not smart for leaving my baby with my boyfriend at the time. I was ashamed to go outside. I didn't want anyone to see me. I didn't want anyone to see the woman who stayed with her abuser and let her son "allegedly "be killed. I was tired of people asking me what happened. The truth is I don't know what happened. I know what was alleged during the two murder trials, but that was all I knew.

The people of the town forgot that we are all sinners and all sin is the same. They forgot about their skeletons in the closet. Just because people knew about her sins in the open didn't mean that others didn't have hidden sin. They don't know the cost the woman paid for that alabaster box. She endured being publicly known as being a sinful woman.

People often want the belongings but don't know the cost the person had to pay outside of money. If people knew the cost some people paid to be where they are it is likely they would not be so envious. Everyone is not meant to travel the same path because everyone is not built to endure the same journey. Some people will spread the negative information about you just because they want what you have or don't want you to have it either.

To me, I am just an ordinary person. Some say to me that I am very successful. I had a person tell me that they wanted to be more like me and leave a legacy like me. I thought to myself you have no idea what it cost me to get here. I do have degrees, bestselling books, and a state job, van, etc. People may look at my life and think that I have it all together, but I do not. I struggle each day as others do.

If people only knew the hell I had to go through to get the little bit of success now they wouldn't be envious. I've been in the newspapers, blogs, magazines, and on radio shows but people do not realize it's to talk about the loss of my child, surviving domestic violence, two nervous breakdowns, suicide attempts and many other things.

You don't know the true cost of getting to where I am.

I cried many nights telling God that I didn't think I was going to make it. God told me that I would make it if I turned my life back over to HIM. After self-destructing from 2001-2003, I renewed my relationship with Jesus Christ. I've been saved since I was 15 years old, but I lost my way. After coming out of the streets partying, I knew that I had to make a change. I recognized, just like the woman with the alabaster box did, that I had to get to Jesus. I didn't care what others thought about me I knew Jesus still loved me.

I had to get back to Jesus, or I was going to die spiritually and perhaps physically from my depression over the loss of my son. Much like the woman with the alabaster box I knew the wrong I was doing and wanted to repent.

The woman with the alabaster box knew Jesus and wanted to meet him and repent. She didn't care what anyone thought about her. She already had a terrible reputation so to her there wasn't any other choice but to get to Jesus. She was bold enough to go to Simon the Pharisee's house without invitation! In those days it just wasn't done. No one dared to go to Simon's house without him asking. To show up at someone's house without an invitation could have dire consequences.

The woman didn't care. She knew she had to get to Jesus at any cost. It was worth dying for. In some cases, people don't realize that their soul is dead or dying in a world of sin. She knew there had to be a change in her life and that change was to get to Jesus Christ. Unlike some of the people who judged her, she felt sorrow over her sins and repented about her sinful life.

Others felt comfortable in their sin while judging her and made no effort to repent. She knew what she was doing was wrong. Everyone doesn't recognize when they are wrong and living a less than desirable life. Some have no shame about the sin they are committing. I imagine the people in her town didn't have much shame as they contributed to spreading the gossip about the woman. As a result, they failed to repent of their own sins.

This woman wanted to do better, and she wanted to be better. She would get the last laugh as Jesus honored her.

As aforementioned, the woman with the alabaster box was a known sinner. It's different when only you and God know your sins than when you are known for sin; it's an entirely different experience.

This woman must have felt such shame with people knowing her sins or even that people knew anything at all. She lived with that yet said, "I don't care I need to see Jesus." She knew Jesus was the Messiah. She knew what HE taught and knew where to find him. She understood the value *in Jesus Christ*.

She broke open the alabaster box and used the oil to anoint Jesus. She understood that Jesus was of more importance than anything or anyone else.

Her critics, the disciples and other onlookers, lacked humility. They were often arrogant and self-centered. Simon invited Jesus to his home for a meal and yet didn't honor him and show him the hospitality that was due to the Almighty. She served the Lord with humility. She most notably served HIM by drying his feet with her hair. They could not have honored Jesus in the way that the woman did.

I found it interesting that Jesus honored a woman who wasn't afraid to humble herself. The woman's name was never mentioned, but she didn't do it for the honor. She did everything to glorify the Almighty. The Lord spoke to the woman and told her that her sins were forgiven. That must have been quite a load off her shoulders. Imagine being talked about by an entire town, and then you are made new. That is quite a change. I imagine that after leaving from seeing Jesus, she cared less about what people back home thought about her. She knew Jesus loved her and forgave her and that was key to her freedom.

It took me many years to realize that Jesus loves me regardless of my downfalls. HE already knew I would make mistakes. HE already knew what types of mistakes I would make. HE already knew people were going to talk about me. HE already knew it all. There was no need for me to be ashamed and wasting all that time instead of repenting, accepting the forgiveness and moving on with my life.

One of my priorities is the advancement of Christ and His Gospel. I must let people know that God is real, and HE loves all of us. Often people hear too much about if you sin you go to hell. You will burn in the lake of fire.

While it is true that if a person does not repent of their sins, they will go to hell, that's not the only part of the bible. People need to know who Jesus Christ is. They need to know that HE loves them.

I hope my life shows someone that redemption through Jesus Christ is possible.

HE set me free.

Letisha Galloway is a speaker, poet, and book coach. She uses her witty style of humor to bring laughter into the lives of many.

She obtained a Bachelor of Science degree in Criminal Justice, a Master of Science degree in Administration of Human Service, and a Master of Science degree in Administration of Justice from Wilmington University. She is also a Senior Social Worker/Case Manager in Delaware.

Surviving domestic violence herself, Letisha is a strong advocate for change and protection for those who feel they have no voice. She is regularly involved in bringing awareness to domestic violence and child abuse. Additionally, she advocates for ending hunger and homelessness.

From Woodstown, New Jersey and currently residing in Delaware, Letisha is a Best-Selling author of more than 15 books and is a contributor to all three TESTIFY books.

Letisha is the mother of one, a son named Jordan, who is resting peacefully in the arms of God.

Contact her on Facebook and Twitter or:
Email: letisha.nicole@gmail.com
Website: www.letishagalloway.com

MY BOX OF ALABASTER
MINISTER ALMENA MAYES

An *Alabaster* is a semi-precious stone; used to make containers which would hold only the most expensive and precious contents.

When the contents were extremely precious, the makers would work the stone in such a way that the only way to empty it would be to break the container. We have heard of the woman who anointed the feet of Jesus with oil she poured from a box of alabaster. However, when I think of my alabaster box, my mind tends to envision something a little different.

My alabaster box consists of my relationship with the Most High. There are so many reasons why this relationship has served as my protection, my caretaker, my fortress, and my resting place. You have no idea the cost of the oil in this alabaster box.

Initially, my relationship with God was surface. It was the thing we "did" in my family. We looked really good going to church every Sunday. I stood up and said my Bible verses with the Sunday school students. I served on the youth missionary. I sang in the youth choir. And, I even served as the pianist for the choir. I went through the motions for many years; never knowing the fullness of God or what being His child really meant. I had His love, I truly believed that, but I was not in a place where I had learned to fully reciprocate that love. It wasn't until I faced sexual abuse that I learned how God's love could keep me.

Many times, I found myself alone and feeling as if there was no one who loved me. I felt dirty and used. I believed that I had nowhere to go and no one to turn to. This was when the love of my heavenly Father surrounded me. He protected me against the feelings that would have led me to suicide. He alone told me that my life had meaning and purpose. He strengthened my mind, body, and spirit. I had no idea, but God had begun to craft my box. He started restoring me without me even knowing it.

My alabaster box was crafted through many different events in my life. Some of them were good. The birth of my three children and watching them grow and flourish comes to mind when I think of the good times. However, there were some trying times as well. For instance, the dissolution of my sixteen-year marriage was one of the hardest times. What I realized is that to craft something extraordinary there has to be an extraordinary process.

I expected my life to be easier once I accepted my Lord and Savior. Boy, was I wrong! It seemed like the moment I said,

"Okay, God. I'm yours, and my life is in your hands," all hell broke loose! A diagnosis of Multiple Sclerosis (MS), a divorce, a repossession of my car and loss of my home all took place within a year! I began to feel like I was Job. Many nights I cried into my pillow, hoping my children wouldn't hear, waiting for God to answer my questions... *What did I do Lord? What did I do to deserve this punishment? Why am I being chastised so severely? How can I make this right?*

Eventually, I stopped asking questions and trusted God to take care of me and to meet all of my needs according to his purpose for and promise on my life. This, I found, was what God wanted from me. Complete and total surrender to Him was what He desired. I came to realize that as I went through my issues, I still thought it was my job to fix everything. I worked extreme hours, spending time away from children who needed their mother; trying to make enough money to make ends meet. I constantly worried about what would happen tomorrow, and I continuously questioned God rather than trusting Him and His wisdom for my life.

I had been going through the motions but not truly trusting Him. What he revealed to me was that I mourned situations that he intentionally removed from me. The funny thing was He only did what I had requested. In my prayer, I had asked that He remove from me anything that was not of Him.

He answered that prayer! The 16-year marriage I was in was not one he had ordained. In fact, I had not consulted Him whatsoever. Being unhappy, abused and cheated on was not what He desired for me. It was what I chose for myself!

Sometimes we are so anxious to "have someone" or to show the world that we are "worthy" that we enter into covenants with people God had not designed for our lives. This is what I had done. I had given my life over to one who should have never been a part of it. The human desire to be a part of something can cloud our judgment. It can make us forget that we are already a part of something. God gave me a "not so gentle" reminder that He was in control. When I surrendered to that control, things began to change.

God revealed to me that my relationship with Him had to come first. It had to be the primary focus of my life. In doing this, aligning my focus with His, I would be able to see his path for me. My low self-esteem, low self-worth, and low focus had brought me to an even lower place in my life. God wanted to elevate me, but to do so He first needed me to look up. He needed me to lift my eyes towards the hills from which comes our help. He needed me to look to Him and fully trust Him as the author of my destiny.

Finally, my box was crafted. My relationship with God had been solidified. I trusted Him, believed His word, stepped out on my faith and did things I never thought were possible. In this box of alabaster, I placed all my hopes, my dreams, my heart's desires and my reservations. I gave God my life, my children, my ministry and my relationships. In this alabaster box, I placed everything that was dear to me; everything I valued.

Unfortunately, I still didn't truly understand the value of the alabaster box. Yes, I had surrendered myself to God. Yes, I truly trusted Him. And, yes, I was ready to live the life He had planned for me while I yet rested in my mother's womb. At least... I thought so! I had my beautiful alabaster box, and I was ready to face the world. What I had not realized is that the value of the box is not evident while it is intact.

I had to break the box!

For a moment, let's revisit the biblical account of the Alabaster Box, The Anointing of Jesus. No one cared about the value of the fragrance in the alabaster box until it was broken. All of a sudden, everyone had something to say about how wasteful it was to anoint Jesus' feet with the oil. The oil sat in the box, probably for years, and no one even knew what it smelled like. They hadn't even thought about it. It wasn't until it was opened and being poured that people began to smell just how wonderful the fragrance was and talk about it.

While I did my mess, all my "good stuff" was safe in my alabaster box. It was protected from the world and from me. However, nothing changed. My hopes didn't materialize. My dreams didn't come true. My ministry didn't flourish, and my life was still floundering. I had to break the box! God revealed to me that I had to live a life of brokenness for Him. I had to be unafraid to break the box He had built for me. I had to believe and know that our relationship was solid. I had to pour out my oil! I took my most precious things and laid them at His feet, and He blessed me for it!

Don't be afraid to break your box! The world may call you crazy, scholars may call you stupid, and your family may never understand. *You are your alabaster box!* You contain the oil that the world needs.

Break the box, and you will find the fullness of your purpose and the promise on your life.

Almena L. Mayes is an associate minister at Coley Springs Missionary Baptist Church in Warrenton, N.C. She is currently serving under watch care at the Dream Center in Atlanta, Georgia. Born in Paterson N.J and raised in Warrenton, NC she sees herself as a city girl living a country girl's life. She is the mother of three beautiful adults and has three wonderful grandchildren.

Mena, as she is called by friends and family, attended North Carolina Agricultural and Technical State University where she studied Communications and Guilford College where she earned a degree in English with a concentration in writing.

In addition to writing, Mena is a singer and songwriter. She truly believes that God's message may be packaged differently for different people, but the message is always the same; He saves, He heals, and He restores.

Practical application of spiritual principles is Mena's mission in life. *"If we can't make the message relevant then people will not embrace it."* She feels a responsibility to present the message of God's never-ending love to all people in a judgment-free zone. "We all have issues, we all have problems, but by being transparent to ourselves and God, we can grow beyond them."

She is an author, radio host, motivational speaker, and a lifelong cheerleader. Her freshman book, **Just Eat the Beans** was released in January 2016.

Contact her at:
Facebook: JustEattheBeans2016

IN CONCLUSION
MINISTER ANGEL M. BARRINO

Whew! And I've come to pour my praise on Him, like oil from Mary's Alabaster Box... you don't know the cost of the oil in my Alabaster Box.[2]

What a tremendous blessing **TESTIFY: The Praise Literary Collection** has been to me and many others.

Even through all of the challenges, delays, setbacks, health challenges, financial hardships, and numerous spiritual attacks, Abba Father has been gracious, merciful, trustworthy and dependable. He has been true to HIS Word; never leaving me or letting me fall.

My life has been a roller coaster ride for sure; yet, I have been blessed and favored numerous times. Even amid my plethora of mistakes. So imperfect, yes, I am; however, a loving Father reached way down and "brought me of the miry clay." Time after time I broke His heart, and He still welcomed me with open arms—He rescued me and approved me with my disqualified self.

---

[2] CeCe Winans, Alabaster Box, October 19, 1999 Wellspring Gospel

No matter who has turned away from me, rejected me or spoken ill of me Abba Father has been there to assure me that I am still His.

Even in October 2017, when I wanted to give up, say *forget it all,* and commit suicide, He did not allow me to do so. I remember looking at all of the bottles of medication on my desk (more medicine than I've ever been prescribed in my life) and thinking, *No one will care. I can just take them all.*

Then, I remember texting my companion and telling him "goodbye," and he didn't even realize what I was saying. BUT, the spirit of the Holy and Righteous King rose up in me and declared, "You shall live and not die." So, I called one of my besties the next day and told her about it. I also called my spiritual mom, and she said, *"If you ever get to that dark place again, call me. Don't ever let yourself get there again."*

When my income completely stopped, the businesses folded, and I had to walk away from my Multimedia Internet Broadcasting Network, I was heart-broken and wounded. And, when my heart began doing crazy things (missing beats, pausing, and off-rhythm), there was numbness on the left side of my body, blood pressure was sky high, still living with excruciating pain throughout my body, a new diagnosis of Diabetes, the Lupus came back, AND the fire became hotter after being ordained a prophetess and minister of the Gospel, still, my Abba Daddy said, *"Trust me… I am with you."*

He carried me through this process. The last five years have been HARD; they've been extremely difficult. Transition after transition left me nearly homeless and in poverty, living with other people, from couch to couch, on the floor, sometimes wondering what I might eat from day to day—situations many did not know about—BUT GOD! I continued to show up and encourage others, despite my own pain, and He was still there within all of it.

I cried through it... prayed through it... fasted through it... I was told, "Go work here. Go work there."

Do this. Do that.

People didn't realize how many job applications I completed daily, only to receive rejection after rejection. Many gave up on me, turned their backs on me, and treated me as if I were a complete burden and disgrace to them. BUT, my Father was faithful. He kept saying, *"Trust me... you are healed, I am with you."*

It didn't look like it.

I was scared, filled with anxiety. Every time I said, "Lord I give up. I will discontinue Alabaster Box; I won't even publish it," He said, *"Oh, yes you will. You will finish everything. You will not give up. Get up and do what I've called you to do."*

He had not given me a spirit of fear or anxiety, yet He allowed each level of testing because He knew that I could handle it. He prepared me and equipped me in the process. I know Him to be a deliverer, a healer, a provider, a protector, and my FATHER.

You see, this is not just another publication. The prophetic implications of this series caused me to LIVE OUT each one of them. That is why it has taken so long to complete. That is why it seemed like it wasn't moving. That is why satan got angry and began hurling fiery darts even more than I've ever experienced in my life.

This series isn't about me, nor is it solely about the authors; it is about the Father's glory being revealed and His Kingdom being expanded. It is about healing, restoration, deliverance, true repentance and heartfelt change in the lives of His children.

So, you see, it could only be released in His timing and according to the completion of events leading up to each release. Prophetic fulfillment has come through each edition, and this is the year of the Prophetic Scribe. This series was released into His hands from the beginning and many disconnected from the project and me. I understand *why*, and I am okay with what has taken place.

With the first book, **Testimonials,** miracles were manifested. With the second book, **Unmerited Favor,** many of the authors, including myself, were placed in unusual circumstances in which WE had to COMPLETELY rely upon God's favor. And, with this third, and final book of the "TESTIFY" series, *oh my goodness*, what a tremendous fight through **Worship** this has been. I had to learn to trust Abba Father in a way like never before, and He clearly stated, *"Worship me through all of this. Do not stop worshipping me."*

My prayer is that you, the reader, will be tremendously blessed and that you will receive your healing for whatever need you may have.

You may be broken, downtrodden, and feel completely alone; but, let me tell you one thing: Abba Father is with you, and He is concerned about every need you have.

Find Him through these words. Seek His face, and do not be afraid; for He will never leave you. His promises are true, and they will come to pass for you. Spend the time in His Word and His presence to receive His strength and instructions for your every move. He will answer.

The popular song, *Alabaster Box* by CeCe Winans and the Bible story have never been more real to me than they are now. Throughout this experience, the following scriptures have been my foundation. Prayerfully, they will be a blessing to you:

Psalm 23	Isaiah 54
Psalm 91	Joshua 1-3
Psalm 119	Jeremiah 29
Psalm 42	Proverbs 3
Isaiah 43	

Thank you for your support and *we love you*...

Beloved Reader...

Beloved readers... again, we thank the Father for you and your support. Our desire is to see you and your families blessed, all people connected to you healed, and you living victoriously according to the Father's Word and His promises. We decree and declare that you shall live and not die, you shall walk in victory, and you shall accomplish all that He desires for you.

Pray the following prayer with us ...

"Father God in the name of Jesus your word tells me to seek the Kingdom first and its righteousness and all things will be added unto me.

Lord change my mind! Help me to think like a champion, a winner, as an overcomer! Help me to step up to the plate and win the fight! I Thank you today for the peace that surpasses all understanding, for the joy of the Lord is my strength! Your word declares that if I decree a thing, it shall be established.

Today I'm making my confession known and I decree and declare Divine Health, Wealth, Happiness, Prosperity and Increase in every area of my life. I thank you for unmerited favor and mercy that covers me and protects me from the world economy what man deems as impossible. I thank you for the many blessings that You have bestowed upon Your chosen people, the seed of Abraham, your beloved children of the Most-High God.

You came so that I would have life and life more abundantly and I receive it by faith and by boldly declaring it shall be done in Jesus name.

I confess with my mouth that I am redeemed from the curse of sickness, poverty, fear, worry and stress. I rely on the Kingdom of God to supply all of my needs according to your riches. I rejoice that Your promise to Abraham to make him a great nation and that all the people of the earth would be blessed through his descendants extends to me and my family. Father in the name of Jesus I make my petitions known that you will bless me indeed and enlarge my territory so that I would be a blessing to others.

For you have given me power to get wealth and success. Since there is no failure in you, there is no failure in me. No longer do I have to borrow, but I will be a lender to man nations. I declare that I am the head and not the tail, above and not beneath and I take authority over what belongs to me that has been held up.

I decree declare that the wealth of the sinner is being transferred to your servant and I lack nothing. Everything that has been stolen, held up and held back is being released and restored according to your Word beyond measure. Father, just as you blessed Potiphar's house for Joseph's sake, I pray and release the same blessing over my household. I decree and declare the release of divine favor in my life endeavors and everything that concerns me.

I declare supernatural favor with my associates, my enemies, my haters, my boss and everything that concerns me. I speak to my hands and declare that everything I touch will prosper, succeed and multiply. Thank you for superabundance and overflow. I expect supernatural favor and provision in my life and in my finances now in Jesus name. Where there is lack in my life I speak overflow, where there is debt I speak cancellation, where there is sadness, I speak joy, where there is discord I speak peace.

Father, I decree and declare that I am blessed with financial prosperity and stability and that I want for nothing because you are supplying all of my needs. Your Word declares that the blessing of the Lord makes one rich, and He adds no sorrow with it. I ask you today to perfect those things that concern my life, my worship to you, my family my ministry, my business and my destiny and purpose.

I thank you in advance for enlarging my territory and increasing my coast, thank you for unspeakable joy, mental peace, and prosperity that is overflowing in abundance following me all the days of my life, and in those lives that are connected to me.

In Jesus' name...

Amen"

Submitted by:
Elder Nataisha Dickey-Pointzes;
MS, BSW, QPMH, CSAC-I
Psychosocial Rehabilitation Program Director
Minister, Author, Speaker, Women's Advocate

Contact her on Facebook

PUBLISHER:

Angel B. Inspired Inc.
Greensboro, NC 27406
(704) 978-8679
www.angelbinspired.com
angelbinspired@gmail.com
rehobothrestoredintl@gmail.com

Facebook: www.facebook.com/angelbinspired2
Twitter: www.twitter.com/angelbinspired
LinkedIn: www.linkedin.com/in/angelbarrino
Instagram: www.instagram.com/angelbinspired

Cover and Interior Design:
DHBonner Virtual Solutions LLC
www.dhbonner.net

www.ingramcontent.com/pod-product-compliance
Lightning Source LLC
Chambersburg PA
CBHW070524100426
42743CB00010B/1945